The Guide To Being A Modern Witch

Ji-hoon K. Kim

All rights reserved. Copyright © 2023 Ji-hoon K. Kim

COPYRIGHT © 2023 Ji-hoon K. Kim

All rights reserved.

No part of this book must be reproduced, stored in a retrieval system, or shared by any means, electronic, mechanical, photocopying, recording, or otherwise, without written permission from the publisher.

Every precaution has been taken in the preparation of this book; still the publisher and author assume no responsibility for errors or omissions. Nor do they assume any liability for damages resulting from the use of the information contained herein.

Legal Notice:

This book is copyright protected and is only meant for your individual use. You are not allowed to amend, distribute, sell, use, quote or paraphrase any of its part without the written consent of the author or publisher.

Introduction

This comprehensive guide provides beginners with an introduction to the mystical world of witchcraft and magick. It covers a wide range of topics, from defining what magick and Wicca are to explaining the importance of maintaining a Book of Shadows for documenting one's magical journey. The guide emphasizes the role of intention in magical practices and explores the concept of individual agency in shaping one's destiny.

Readers are introduced to practical aspects of magick, including daily spells and rituals that can be easily incorporated into their lives. Green magic and kitchen witchery are discussed, along with the use of herbs in spellwork. The guide also delves into the significance of tools like altars, candles, crystals, and cauldrons in magical practices.

Protection spells and rituals are covered in detail, providing readers with the knowledge and techniques to safeguard themselves energetically. The guide also addresses the importance of discernment in identifying and dealing with charlatans who misuse magic.

Furthermore, the guide explores divination methods such as clairvoyance, crystal ball scrying, and tarot card reading, empowering readers to develop their psychic abilities. It also offers insights into connecting with angels, deities, animals, and spirits, emphasizing trust and intuition as essential components of these interactions.

Throughout the guide, practical spells for various purposes, including love, money, and health, are provided, making it a valuable resource for those looking to integrate magick into their daily lives.

Contents

Chapter 1 Fourth Dimensional Circle Time 1
What is Magick? 3
What is Wicca? 3
Chapter 2 Your Book of Shadows 4
Daily Helpful spells 6
But First Coffee Spell 7
Restart Your Day 9
Do-Over Spell 10
Chapter 3 Green Magic 11
Kitchen Witchery 12
Magical Herbs 14
Daily Food Blessing 15
Chapter 4 Intention 17
We are not pawns 19
Chapter 5 The Universe and Dimensions 20
Chapter 6 99.99% Magic 22
Chapter 7 Understanding Frequencies 25
"Your daily life is your temple and your religion" 30
Chapter 8 Tools of the Trade 31
ALTARS 33
Travel Altar 33
Candles 34
Simple Daily Candle Spell 36
Chapter 9 Cauldrons 37

Daily Goodbye Bad Things Spell	37
Chapter 10 Crystals/Rocks	40
Chapter 11 Protection	43
Candle Protection	45
Invoking a circle for protection	45
Visualization Protection	45
Sound Protection	45
Super Divine Protection Prayer	46
Chapter 12 COVENS AND FRIENDS	47
Chapter 13 Clairvoyance	49
Chapter 14 CRYSTAL BALL SCRYING	52
Chapter 15 Tarot and Oracle Cards	54
Chapter 16 Clairaudience	57
Chapter 17 Clairsentience	59
Chapter 18 Inner Magic	61
Outer Magic	62
Love Magic	63
Chapter 19 5 Step Spell To Magically Get What You Want	65
Chapter 20 Spell Step 1	70
Step 1: Exercise	71
Imagine	71
Chapter 21 The Triangle Check	73
Chapter 22 Spell Step 2	76
Chapter 23 Spell Step 3	80
Chapter 24 Spell Step 4	83
Chapter 25 Spell Step 5	86
Keys to Supercharge Your Magic	88

"Even the least among you can do what Ihave done and even greater things."..........90
Chapter 26 Spells/Affirmations 91
Where's my Darn Wish? 94
Chapter 27 Glamour Spell 96
Chapter 28 Invisibility Cloak 99
Chapter 29 CHARLATONS 102
Chapter 30 I need a Hex or a Jinx Spell 105
Easy Cord Cutting Spell' 106
Binding Spell 107
Chapter 31 I NEED REVENGE 109
It's Curse Time! 110
The ULTIMATE CURSE 113
Could You Be Cursed? 116
Chapter 32 Portal Jumping 118
Chapter 33 Cleansing 120
INVOKING PROTECTION CLEANSE 121
Super Protection Spell to Banish UnwantedSpirits 121
Clearing Spell for Home or Objects 122
Clearing Yourself 122
Chapter 34 Expanding Your Power 124
Chapter 35 Earthing 126
Building Power with Self Love 128
Chapter 36 CLEARING OLD TAPES 131
Daily Easy Sticky Note Spell 135
Chapter 37 How to Talk to Angels, Deities, Animals andthe Deceased 136
Sixth Sense Communication 136
Chapter 38 Honing Your Gift Through Meditation 138

Chapter 39 Recognizing Voices in Meditation	141
Chapter 40 Strengthening your Sixth Sense	144
Chapter 41 Angels and Deities	147
Chapter 42 Trust	152
Chapter 43 Talking to Animals	154
Chapter 44 Wild Animal Messengers	156
Understand Animal Messages	157
Chapter 45 Power Animals	159
Chapter 46 Talking to the Dead	160
Chapter 47 Ghosts and Spirits	164
Ghosts	165
Chapter 48 Simple Useful Spells	169
New Moon Money Magic	169
Good Morning Spell	170
Wash Away Troubles	170
To Bring Love to You	172
To Bring Health to a Friend	172
The Great Calling	173

Chapter 1 Fourth Dimensional Circle Time

As a guide to moving through this book, we're going to need to step out of linear 3-D time here and instead enter into *magic time.* We will be entering the fourth dimensional circle time where anything is possible.

I suggest you approach this magical awakening in an attuned personal way for you. Look through the chapters in the table of contents and see what sparks your interest and move to those first.

I think three of the major things that draw most beings to awaken their magical abilities and which I will teach you are how to:

1. Make material things appear in your reality and things like love, success, and health.

2. Connect to the divine source and invoke and communicate with spirits, animals, Angels, and the dead.

3. Have fun with magical stuff to liven up my life.

While I will touch on the aspects of essential tools used as a way to magnify your energy – lets never forget you have the POWER within you – your heart energy is your built-in wand, you need nothing other than your joy and intention to make things appear like magic here and now.

If you practice a religion that bans 'Witchy' things, you can skip the whole ritual ceremony part. None of the tools are needed; they are just aids in helping you magnify your energy. But, again, you can do this yourself. You are the source of the power because the source is in you.

You may not remember how to wield it, but that's why you're here.

In some of the chapters, you will whiz through no problem, others may move more slowly, and you might feel stuck. If you move into part of this information that upsets you or you don't agree with, or that is difficult - *skip it* - come back to it when you're ready.

Sometimes certain information can be overwhelming, and you may need to go slowly. Many things you will learn will require you to break long-held beliefs and paradigms.
Please go with the pace that's good for you!
You don't have to race to any place, and you don't have to finish this book in a day, a week, or a month. You don't have to complete any of the exercises if you don't want to; this should be a fantastic, fun time where you get to play and reawaken some of the best parts of yourself.

What is Magick?

Magick is using your force to create things out of the ethers and pull it into reality. It deals with your personal evolution and power as well as creating things on the daily. You want a good job? Use magick. You want to enchant a new lover? Use magick. How about health and abundance? Yep, you want to use magick.

Any time you say an affirmation you are using magick. This spelling of magick was used to delineate it from *performance magic* that a magician may exhibit in a show.

What is Wicca?

Wicca is a new growing religion that was created by a man in the 1950's named Gerald Gardner. It is influenced by pre-Christian beliefs and practices of Western Europe that affirms the existence of a supernatural power – or magic – and believes in a male and female deity. It emphasizes ritual observance of seasonal life cycles and the love of nature.

Unlike Witchcraft, which is a craft and practice – Wicca is a religion. Wicca idolizes a female fertility god and a horned male hunter god and is a formal religion. It focuses on ritual and often utilizes pagan traditions.

Often working in covens members are entered through an initiation ritual. As coven members master the practice of magick and rituals they pass through higher degrees of initiation to become a priest or priestess.

Thus Wicca might best be describes as a modern religion based on ancient Witchcraft traditions. Many Wiccans also consider themselves Witches and practice Witchcraft.

Chapter 2 Your Book of Shadows

As we advance, you will be acquiring a lot of knowledge and especially personal expertise about yourself and your powers. One of the most critical tools in any magical person's practice is known as the BOOK OF SHADOWS.

This is the classic reference to the very personal journals kept to document progress by a magical person.

You can call it anything and decorate it in any way that appeals to you. You can use any paper or notebook you currently own, or you can purchase one that really calls to you.
If you are a crafty Witch, you can make your very own book and decorate it, as you like to really personalize it—some people like

darker themes, others like fairies or nature themes. Do whatever makes you feel good and keep it to yourself.

This should not be confused with the GRIMOIRE, a book where you keep spells and affirmations you have gathered MINUS your own experiences with said affirmations or spells. A grimoire is similar to a cookbook of recipes but only spells.

You can have both books or just keep all your magical experiences in one place, your choice. But choose something you like now, so as we move ahead, you don't miss anything, and you document your awakening!

Daily Helpful spells

Throughout this book I will sprinkle in daily spells and situational spells that even a beginner can do easily with no tools.
First let's talk about what a spell is.
A spell is an intention pulled into the physical.
Thus you channel an idea from your imagination and you pull that wish down into reality.
My dear magical aspirants you have been doing spells forever. When you write something down on paper, you bring it into the third dimension, and when you use a third dimensional item like a pen or computer to write it down – by the very act of spelling it out in the physical form you have created a spell!
Spelling is a spell.
So now let's do spells on purpose to get what we want.

I think one of the most delightful parts of practicing the craft of intention or witchcraft is in daily practice. It's our everyday little moments that make up our lives. Filling them with intention and our force – or magick - brings bliss to our life.

Magick doesn't have to be big and complicated to be powerful.
First let's remember that you are in charge.
If you are a Lazy Witch, like me, you may be more minimalistic. Sometimes I want to perform a big ceremony to celebrate a special event and then sometimes I just need to get it done now - because I'm busy man!
The truth is whatever you decide so it will be.

You can just declare whatever your intention is and that will be your magic carpet reality! You'll see – Intention is everything in magic.

But First Coffee Spell

It is the start to a new wonderful day. Let's get you on the right vibration. Grab your drink of choice and let's intend your day right from the beginning.

Sit in front of your cup of coffee/or tea/ or smoothie. Take a deep breath. Know that you are in charge of how your day will go.

Take your spoon and spin it around three times in your cup and stare into it as you say these words:

> "I'm thrilled about this wonderful day
> I'm in charge and the world doth obey
> My day is amazing beyond imagination
> I'm filled with joy and inspiration
> So be it."

Another version of this morning spell is to use it as an intention focus to will your desire into your life.

As you stir your coffee or morning drink of choice - state what you want to happen in your life.

"I intend to be successful beyond my imagination. So be it!"

"I pull in money unexpectedly in divine ways all day today. So be it!"

"Wherever I go I find joy. So be it!"

"My body is balancing and restoring its divine perfection. So be it!"

"I am grateful for my health and abundance may it multiply in a divine way. So be it!

Restart Your Day

Being magical helps with many things. Some of the daily things we all run into are problematic encounters - or what I call the bad vibes. Maybe it's a fight with someone we love, maybe we overslept and are running late for work, or maybe we got no sleep at all. Maybe it's a whole lot of bat crap crazy.
It's a bad start.
So let's change that.
When we get hit with a bunch of low vibes, we can carry that bad energy with us through our entire day and that is just a waste of a good day. We need not wait until Monday or Jan. 1st to begin afresh when we feel like we need a new start. We can change our vibration by taking control of the moment and demanding a restart right now.

Here's an easy spell to get your day back on track. Come on, let's get that yucky energy off of you and have a fabulous day.

Do-Over Spell

First pick something you can do to signal to yourself that you are doing a Do-Over spell. It can be anything such as a quick walk, lighting a candle or simply stopping and taking three deep breaths. I like to turn around counter clockwise three times as if I'm winding back time.
Once you have your symbolic gesture, then you declare what you want – *to let the past go and restart your vibration.*
Say this:

> "What happened is done and gone
> I let go of the past and move on
> All good vibes are coming my way
> It's going to be a fabulous day!
> So mote it be"

Chapter 3
Green Magic

M uch of the joy of practicing Witchcraft is reconnecting with nature. Working with herbs in cooking or gardens is a beautiful way to bring daily magic into your life. Besides the beauty of plants and flowers, they make us feel better when we are around them because they are filled with the divine frequency.
Most Witchcraft practices involve nature and working with natural elements and tools.
Being in the forest, around streams and oceans makes you feel alive again. It reminds you that you are part of the bigger picture of Earth. This love affair with nature is one reason why so many magical people identify as Green Witches.

One of the most incredible gifts I believe you will learn during your workings with the green world is how to be present in each moment. The act of nourishing life through gardening is a life lesson any person can enjoy. Putting your hands in the soil and integrating yourself into the thirteen realm of plants and flowers will illuminate your life.

There are hundreds of paths and journeys and titles magical people use to identify themselves. In truth, many of us have multiple gifts or callings within the craft so please know that you can identify or not identify as any kind of Witch or many all at once.
Know that when you get excited about learning more of a certain path that you should go research it on a deeper level as it may be your particular gift. Excitement and curiosity are the hallmark signs that mean - follow me!!
I'm covering many parts of an infinite wisdom so forgive me my brevity on some subjects such as the path of the Green Witch that deserve much more in depth teachings.

The bottom line is joy is a present verb. The craft calls for you to slow down and appreciate daily blessings, be it the moon or the rocks or the candle as it burns in the moment – in the present.

Multi-tasking hurts our minds and spirits. We miss our life, lovers, and important moments as we rush on toward the next barely acknowledged moment. As you learn the craft of magic, you will find yourself drawn to slow down and be present with the now.
To live with full intention it to truly live.
Magic calls you back to living a more sacred connection with nature and yourself and a reason so many magical people identify as Green Witches.

Kitchen Witchery

One of the ways I work daily with the green world is to put magick in my food using herbs and vegetables and fruits.
There is a whole branch of magic dedicated to working with food and if this is your calling you may want to look into the path of the *Kitchen Witch*.

Obviously this is an extensive and exhilarating part of working your magical craft and as I love cooking with magic one on which I could expound an entire book's worth.
Sadly I have to stay brief so I can give you an overview of all the things I want to share.
That said here is my personal favorite spell that I use everyday.
It is a simple but fabulous spell you can do while you cook a meal. The spell enchants your food with magick and intention and thus spreads blessings to all your friends and family who share the meal.

If I cook for myself I infuse my food with love and gratitude, and when I cook for others, I include things that might enchant or help them.

This is how you do it. While you are cutting up your herbs, infuse the food you are preparing with the gifts you want people eating your food to be given. Here's a spell I use as I prepare a magical meal.

I fully suggest that you grow your own herbs when possible, but if not, buy herbs or use herbs you may already have at home. All herbs are magical, but again, if you wish to learn more about being a Green Witch, you can study all the different herbs and choose the ones with specific properties you want to bring in.
Remember if the world of Green Witchery or the path of the Kitchen Witch calls to you there are many nuances to learn but for the sake of simplicity we will start with this list.

Magical Herbs

Marjoram – *Joy, Happiness, Health*
Basil – *Love and Protection*
Sage – *Wisdom and Protection*
Rosemary – *Fame and Luck*
Thyme – *Courage*
Mint – *Money and Travel*
Dill – *Luck*

Pick the herb you want to use (or use any herbs you have on hand.) In this enchantment we will give everyone LOVE.
You can substitute anything you want to share where I use LOVE – such as health, success, joy etc.
Now take the herb and thank it, then gently tear it with your hands into the dish you are making while reciting this spell.

Daily Cooking Spell

"As love I give, so shall I live,
What goes around comes around,
This herb I grind by power of mind,
What had been ground by will be bound.
So mote it be"

Then sprinkle the herbs into the food and spread beautiful magic to everyone that eats it.

This is a lovely ritual you can do at every meal and every day if you want. These simple actions of practicing the craft often bring the greatest joy.
Pausing and appreciating the food you cook and the active blessing of it with intention keeps you in the now.
Being present is a rare gift, but one Witchcraft serves up daily if you practice it.

Daily Food Blessing

The American Indians always blessed their food before they harvested it or ate it. I like to do that too. Gratitude and appreciation are very high frequencies. This is how I bless my food.

Put your plate of food and or drink in front of you and sing the heartnote which is the vowel sound A. It sounds like -

Ahhhhhhhh

Just sing the note over your food.
The heart note raises the frequency and blesses the food.

For the science on this, please check out Dr. Emoto's studies on the effect blessing water does. It literally changes the water crystals into beautiful snowflakes.
Remember, our bodies are made up of almost 70% water, my loves so beauty in beauty out.

Fill yourself with love and gratitude by either singing the heart note or just telling your food and drink out loud that you love it.

I know this sounds cheesy, but love is magic in motion.
Love can create miracles.
True love can cross any bridge.
Right now, magick aside– if you have issues with someone in your life and you just open your heart and reach out to that person with true love – whatever blocks or walls or distance there is between you will melt away.
Love is the center of the spokes of much magic.
If all else fails – reach out in love, and you will succeed. True magic indeed.

Chapter 4
Intention

S o now we begin working with magick instead of just talking about it. Get out your Book of Shadows and let's go.
Ready?
Okay. Now write down the answer to this question on your first page.
What is your dream?
Finished? Great! You just wrote your first entry in your Book of Shadows well done!
So how did that go?
Do you have a dream?
Did you have trouble answering the basic first step to making something manifest? Perhaps you wrote down thirty things you wanted? Well done. Intentions and dreams are a heart calling, it's a deep want or desire filled with love.
An Intention is a spell in itself.

You can't make something happen if you don't know what you want. That's just obvious. So let's go manifest something with magick and see how that might look in the real world.

All my greatest magical manifestations happened with no money despite the fact I kept thinking I had to manifest money to get them. I never manifested money to get them, but I always got them. And you will too!!!!
I wrote this to help all of you magical people get what you want because you can and because you deserve it!!
Everyone can do magick and everyone can control their own destiny.

Magick happens in many ways out of the blue and when you're least expecting it. Almost always it happens in a way you would never expect which is one of the greatest things about working with magic and manifesting.
It truly makes you believe that you made things happen when your wish shows up in odd ways.

I do recommend that you don't be hang out like a fisherman with a lone pole fishing for money all day – set your mind at rest and let the gigantic net of divine possibilities sweep through the universe and align with your intention and pull it in for you!

Lets face it - when we want something we've already tried to get it and it hasn't worked!

If we knew how to get it, we'd have done it. So why do we think we'll know how it is going to work if we don't know? Right? We don't know. So just enjoy the show when your desire does come popping in because it's magnificent to witness!!!!

My dear Witches. It's your day at this amusement park called Earth. What do you want to do? What do you want to achieve or have on this planet?

That's the real question and the most complex question, but I'm going to help you face that because once you know *what you want*, and have a clear intention, you will be unstoppable.

Many people *believe they want money*, but money is energy like gravity is energy, just as love is energy – *money is energy* – It's transference energy, more like communication.

You don't love communication, do you? No!
You love the feeling of intimacy with somebody you adore that authentic communication brings, or that feeling of being seen by a kindred spirit when honest communication occurs. Still, you don't *love communication* – just as you don't love money - *you love what money brings*.

Once you decide what you truly love, what excites you and has you jumping out of bed in the morning then the actual *making it appear into your reality is the easy part.*

We are not pawns
in the chess game of life
We are the mover of the pieces.

White Eagle

Chapter 5 The Universe and Dimensions

W elcome to the third dimension conscious weaver!
As we awaken more of our powers, I also want to give you a firm foundation and deep roots.
Knowledge of how the universe and frequencies work will benefit your craft. Many people don't create the magick they desire because they don't believe or understand how it's happening in our free will zone. Oh, such an unlimited topic, but for our needs of creating magic, let me start with these foundational truths.
There are thirteen dimensions.

The ODD dimensions are where we free souls live and create with our FREE WILL. Currently, you are a magical being able to create what you love because you have choices, and this is a free will dimension. (The Third duh.)

The EVEN dimensions are not free will zones; they are SET. They are *Foundations of the Universe*. Angels and Deities live in these even dimensions and hold the fabric of the science of the universe. The second dimension is gravity, the fourth dimension is time, the sixth dimension is geometry, and the eighth is music. I can only channel up to the eighth dimension, so I don't know what the tenth and twelfth-dimensional columns are yet.

That said, I hope you understand that as a free will magical being, you get to create what you want with the "tools" of the universal from the even dimensions that hold up always.

Let's look at this. We've been using the ART and FREE WILL part in magic and Witchcraft for centuries – but the new understanding of frequencies and how they affect creation in the free will zones is relatively new.

Just as gravity is always happening , so too is the law of affinity on this planet.

Chapter 6 99.99% Magic

Creating what we call magick in the third dimension is not a problem of our ability it's a problem of our belief system. We get caught in the minutia of our human lives when we are cosmic beings having a focused perspective in this dimension. Then sometimes the magic bleeds through and we remember…

Let's hear what a real smarty had to say about it:

Einstein said we could study all the quarks and leptons that make up what we know as MATTER down to the tiniest parts – but science (until recently with the God Particle discovery) we don't know anything of the ever-creative pulsing immortal space that makes up 99.99% percent of everything and us too.

Einstein mused the space must be God.

Think about that. You are hardly any bit of *matter* at all.

You are mostly space made up of space.

99.99 percent space that is connected and divine and in all of us!!

The point is we are all connected and have access to this miraculous space. The universal space is our connection to all other things and communication as well. We have the Internet inside us. To top this all off – the rest of you that shows up as a body (or matter) is like a cherry size to the Earth.

That little part that is matter that we see as matter is also magical beyond comprehension. Did you know that the cells you are born with are already a billion years old?

It's true! The cells and frequencies that make up YOU in the third dimension are entirely immortal and mutable at your will. Let's recap – as a human, you are mostly space – 99.99% space and a minimal amount of material that we will call your body. Your body is born with matter made up of cells that are already a billion years old.

Thus the need to enter the magical mind! It makes no sense to me why our bodies fall apart and die in a hundred years when most of us are made up of immortal stardust, and the rest of us is already a billion years old… third-dimensional mind thought, perhaps? Isn't that mind-blowing? Perhaps our mind has been closed, as Aldous Huxley said in The *Doors of* Perception.

> "There are things known,
> and there are things unknown,
> and in between are
> the doors of
> Perception."

Aldous Huxley

The gist of this for those that haven't read the book is that perhaps we are infinite beings that have been squished into third-dimensional bodies that need human things such as sleep, water, food, sex, etc. and the brain acts as a barrier/funnel which will only allow enough information to keep us eating breathing and mating, in other words, to survive in this dimension."

Religious experiences, great loves, and hallucinogenic trips have revealed those things outside the perimeters of the doors. What we know for sure is that we are filled with the divine God particle energy, and we came the furthest from our absolute power to come to the third dimension and have a human experience.

Gravity, taxes, and death – good grief!! So how do we *Tread lightly* as Huxley also suggested? (Which in my lingo is saying *stay high frequency* from which all good things will be magnetically drawn.) Tread lightly friends. Life was not meant to be easy; it was meant to be a day camp. Go play and get dirty, maybe scoffed up a little. Be kind along the way and find things to be passionate about and appreciate your playmates because everyone goes home at the end of the summer.

Chapter 7 Understanding Frequencies

I'm going to keep this very complex subject as simple as possible. In 3-D terms *frequency* is used as a measurement of speed but in universal terms it is used quite differently. The universal science of frequencies is a core language I believe all magical beings should master.

Here are the basics:

1. Everything in the universe is made up of light waves vibrating in the space. All things include all things that have matter such as people, rocks, thoughts and events.
All things with energy or matter are vibrating waves of light.

2. All waves of light hold a frequency level or key frequency. *All waves hold a frequency and this frequency is a measurement of the consciousness of the wave.*
Love and divine frequencies resonate at the high level of 13. Death and violence resonate at a low level of 1. All other frequencies fall

between.

3. Similar frequencies are drawn to each other. The universal law of affinity or in pop culture language - the law of attraction means that like frequencies are drawn to like frequencies.
Like attracts like.

Let's explore how frequencies come into play in life and magic.

You are born made of light waves with the ability to transmit and understand frequencies with your sixth sense and space connection. With this ability you can do what people refer to in the third dimension as magick.

To build your understanding of frequencies I put together a list of common emotions and events that occur in life and I want you to tell me what you think or feel the frequency of each of them are.

Now put your hand over your stomach and take three breaths and ask yourself the frequency level of each of the things. Remember divine filled things are high frequencies and lack of divinity or love is low frequencies.

What number do you get for each of these things listed?

1. Children laughing.
2. Nature.
3. Getting fired from your job.
4. Illness.
5. Getting a promotion.

So now relax and just feel each of these. On a scale of 1-13 with thirteen being God's number according to the Mayans. Where so these events fall frequency level wise?

Most people will put the first two, nature and children laughing at a very high level frequency of 12-13.

How about getting fired from your job?
That feels like a 3 to me – unless you hated the job then it might be more like a 5.

Where would you put getting a serious illness?

Not so loving and joy filled so I would put that down around a level 2. (Other low vibrational things might be anger, a bad car accident or your dog passing away.)

Whereas getting a promotion?
Might be a 9-12 depending on your joy level?

Well done you you're reading frequencies like a pro!!
We already do this as I mentioned when you get that yucky feeling about a place and you don't want to go there for some reason – you're picking up low frequencies.
Or that great looking guy that still feels dark. Yep you're picking up low frequencies.
The outside of something can lie but you can't fake your frequencies.
That's why some people get hired when the interview for a job and others don't. You may think you look prepared and ready but your frequency may be reading NOT READY. So know that frequencies are being read by all of us everyday whether we know it or not and whether we use it to our advantage or not.

Finally lets take those numbers we just came up with for random events and add the law of affinity or the like frequency attracts like frequency part.

Let's use the bad stuff. Examples of low vibes are anger and yelling so we will read that as a level 2. Let's say there are low frequencies around you all the time

coming from you or a partner or coworker. Anyone you hang out with for a long time affects your frequency for the good or bad. This is caused by *sympathetic resonance*. Two energies that co-exist will find a common frequency they can both vibrate at and then go into harmony at that level frequency.
So a friend with great energy and full of joy will pull your energy up to a high level and you will both benefit from resonating together at a higher frequency of joy.

Conversely, if you continue to wallow in a horrible low 2 frequency instead of your natural frequency level (about 8 for most humans) you are lowering your energy to connect comfortably with that low frequency person.
Now let's be aware of what that does to your life and frequency. Now you are hanging out with that cruddy vibe person you feel like crud too. Now you're not zinging in good energy you've had to find an average frequency you can both connect with which means YOU have to go down in frequency. Now what are you creating with the law of affinity when you allow yourself to merge with events and things on that level 2 that resonates with nasty life events and feelings.

Which means you are pulling in rotten 2 stuff like broken hearts, going to jail, losing things you love, car accidents and drug overdoses. 2's travel and magnetize other 2's!! Sounds a lot like a curse right?
But you aren't stuck there.
The only way out is up!

Choosing and being around higher frequencies will lift your frequency from the quicksand crud level on up to the good level -but it will feel difficult to do that.
Low frequencies are mucky, confusing and sap your energy. That said, you must raise your frequency by adding fun and loving things. Working with magic and the tools of Witchcraft based on nature is a

great way to raise your frequency. If you really need a pick up frequency get out in nature and lie down on the grass.
Nature is the highest divine frequency and will help lift your frequency back to your core level.
This may take time.
High frequencies move fast and with ease, low frequencies are sluggish and hard. Depression lives in the low frequencies so you may not feel like doing anything fun or good for you - that's when you must go connect back to nature and infuse your force with the divine frequency.

Okay that's the basics of the law of frequency attunement and if you want more in depth understanding feel free to check out my many books on frequencies including THE FREQUENCY and ADVANCED MANIFESTING.

"Your daily life is your temple and your religion"

Kahlil Gibran

Chapter 8

Tools of the Trade

The many tools used in Witchcraft are as varied as Witches themselves. Depending on what type of Witchcraft you prefer to practice, you will be guided to add different tools to aid your magic. A Kitchen Witch may have herbs and magical recipes, whereas a Pop-Culture Witch may choose to use Harry Potter potions. Some Witches favor bones and blood.

Witchcraft is never-ending and ever fascinating. From singing crystal balls to shaker bottles, there are objects to aid in your craft that you can buy and use if you feel called.
However, wants and needs are different.
I want all of the Harry Potter wands but what I need is different. As you may desire and purchase any number of magical tools down the

line, to begin with, what you need to do magic and learn magic is very simple and requires no purchases.

Other than yourself, you need a notebook (known as your Book of Shadows) and an open mind.
You are ready to practice magic!

As you begin to work with your magic, your true nature will show itself. You will find yourself drawn to learn more about specific types of the craft and how Witches of that type practice. Magick is very personal, and when it is personal, it is much stronger.

That said, some tools are pretty standard in most Witches' worlds, such as candles, crystals, smoke sticks, incense, cauldrons, and an altar.

ALTARS

Altars are your own special area that is dedicated to you and your workings. They are a great thing to incorporate into your life to remind yourself that you are creating your life with intention.

Altars can be filled with many things, but I advise you to include things you love and which bring you joy. Some things I like to include are nature-based, like flowers, or herbs, or crystals. Something you love may include pictures of your loved ones or a favorite pet or deity that you feel a kinship with.

Altars intended to do rituals and spells may contain more private matters and tools, so let's consider altar locations especially if you are still in the broom closet.

You can put your altars in any place you want to spread good magic! One Witch friend mentioned she doesn't like to put her altar in her bedroom because she wants to keep that room clear.

If you intend to do rituals and spells with your altar, you will most likely want to put it in a personal space that only you interact with (if possible.)

You can also choose to have multiple altars, for instance – a protective/love altar as you enter your house or a cooking altar in your kitchen where you use your kitchen Witch skills.

Travel Altar

One of the things I love to do is create mini travel altars to carry with me on vacations or during the day. It is a lovely reminder that I am creating my life and also gives me the ability to connect with my magical side anytime I want. You can bring this to work or anywhere you'd like to keep a little magic at hand.

It's a great creative project and fun too. I use a mint tin and then I decorate it with flowers and other symbols of things I love. Inside I carry a small crystal, incense matches and a candle. I also carry a good luck Wolf charm I was given and some private magical things I've acquired.

Candles

Candles are lovely to work with in your practice. If this type of magic calls to you, then you may like to purchase different colored candles and figurine candles in your magic. Candles are a fantastic way of powering up the fire force and holding the light for your wish.
There are many different schools of thought on which color candle should be used for which workings and at which times. If you find yourself drawn to candle magic, you may want to research which colors work for you and experiment with them.

When I use colored candles I usually equate them to the chakra color I'm working with. I also prefer to use small candles because I want to have the magic work quick and not leave fire burning too long if I need to go out and leave it. The small birthday candle size are perfect for a quick wish ceremony and easy to carry in your travel altar.

Again, as a practical and lazy Witch, I like to make magic work in my life my way.
Some people like to do extensive spells and rituals but I'm just not that gal. I'm the easy-going *get er done t*ype. Remember your craft is your craft.
You do you.

I also love to make my own candles and infuse them with my whole vibe and intention. If you would like to make your own candles it is actually very easy. You can get a starter kit online and start making your own candles right at home on your own stove.
I love putting in fresh herbs, pink peppercorns and crystals or flowers I have. This is also a great place to use scent and add essential oils you prefer and are using in a working. In any case making your own candle is very powerful and fun = double good stuff.

One way in which I use candles is to light them with an intention.
This is a simple yet powerful way to integrate candle magic into your life every day.
I always light candles during the day when I'm writing or just want to bring in magick to my day.
I simply light the candle and say the words or spell or intention I want to cast it with.

Simple Daily Candle Spell

Light the candle and say what you wish to have in your life right now.

A couple sample spells you could use are:

> "With this light, I call in health and joy.
> So mote it be"

> "With this light, I call in beauty and love. So be it."

Remember the power is in you. Declare it so and it is.

What you might intend into your life is endless and unique for you. Just don't waste a candle lighting in the future. Even if the candle is not on your altar or being used in magick practice, still know that each flame holds a wish and take advantage of the element of fire.

If you want to do more ceremonial work with your candles, you can etch something into the candle you want before you burn it: such as – GRATEFUL or LOVE or HEALTH.

Many magical people like to use symbols unique to them and carve them into the candle before lighting, known as sigils.
Sigils are symbolic representations of energy or things that you want to be activated. It is ancient magick and sends messages to your subconscious and the universe to help you manifest.
Another way to use candle magic is to light the candle and meditate on a desire you have. Sit with the energy of the flame and let it symbolize your burning desire.

Chapter 9
Cauldrons

Cauldrons have so many uses, but one reason for certain that a new Witch needs a cauldron is for burning smoke sticks, candles, spells, and incense.

Witches, we need to take care with the fire element, and your cauldron is your best friend for this. Remember safety first wise one!

I prefer a cast-iron cauldron. You might want to buy a couple down the line, but a small one is perfect for keeping your intentions to yourself, if you will.

Daily Goodbye Bad Things Spell

Part of magick is bringing things into your life that you desire, *another part is getting rid of things we don't want.*
Perhaps you are overwhelmed with fear or anxiety or maybe you have a bully on your back.
A simple spell is to write down on a piece of paper that which you

want to get rid of in your life and then burn it in the cauldron and send it away.

Say these words as your paper burns.

> "Bad vibes be gone do as I say
> With this smoke I send you away
> Everything is clear and fine
> My life is happy and divine.
> So be it."

While the words burn, see the thing you want turning to ashes and ceasing to exist in your life. Burned and gone. See ya bad vibes.

Another use for a cauldron that I use daily is for protection when I use my smoke stick. Smoke sticks are excellent clearing tools. When you use your smoke stick for clearing for instance you want to waft it about your home making sure you keep the intention of protection or calling in defense while you walk about your space with it – and your cauldron.

The smoke sticks throw off embers and can be dangerous, so when I clear a room with smoke, I carry the cauldron with me to catch any flying debris and to ensure a safe place to let it burn out.

Again, the use for cauldrons down the line in your practice is endless, so I recommend you get one. I mean, we haven't even touched on potions yet, right? Nothing better than a cauldron for that.

I don't work with many potions myself, so I won't be going into details on this skill. However, there are so many talented Witches in every segment of the community with different expertise, and if you feel drawn to potions, you can find a teacher to help you learn more of this beautiful, magical craft.

Chapter 10
Crystals/Rocks

C rystals are similar to candles in that certain kinds and colors are often associated with different spells or wishes you might want. If you're going to begin with crystals I suggest you go and pick one out that calls to you no matter the color or symbolic meaning it may have. Crystals are living energy, and they will work with you like a friend.

When you go to choose one, pick it up and see how it feels and how it looks.
I always choose crystals and rocks based on their calling to me. I feel that calling inside of myself as a YES in my gut when I hold a particular crystal. You may feel warmth in your hand or feel like you prefer a certain one over another for no reason. Just go with your feeling about a crystal and if you can work with it.

Crystals amplify energy for real. When I was in elementary school, the teacher had me stand up and he had divining rods – which measure energy. He walked toward me, and when he got to about a foot from me the rods opened – meaning they had hit an energy field.

What they had hit was my *Aura*, which is magnetic. We all have this. Our bodies emit an energy field that extends at least six inches from our physical body – more if you are powerful magically.
We all have this, and it is what you experience when someone gets too close to you or gets *in your space,* they have gotten into your body space field which is very vulnerable if the person is not your lover or someone you want that close.

In any case, the divining rods hit my field and opened up when the teacher was a foot away from me. The diving rod had hit my electric field or AURA.
Then the teacher had me hold a large clear crystal, and he walked across the room as far as he could go.
Again he turned to me with the divining rods and started to walk toward me. He took two steps, and the rods sprang open – he was 20 feet away from me, but the rods opened. Why? *Because the crystal amplified my energy that far just holding it.*
Okay, that's just real science.
Now let's take that info and apply it to our magical use of crystals.

Now knowing crystals amplify energy, you can use them in multiple ways in your practice.
You can simply hold them and think of your wish or say an affirmation/prayer/ or spell.
You can use the crystal to meditate with or ask it to help you with a wish you are manifesting because it is living energy. It is alive and has energy. Treat your crystals like friends.
I keep them on my altar and around me on my desk when I write. I also like to take baths with my crystals and peacefully dwell in the

water imagining my wish coming true. Water, of course, is another amplifier of energy so double whammy just lying in the bubbles! Plus, putting crystals in the bath with you is a great way to clear your energy if you've been doing spiritual or divination work.

I like to place a crystal near me to act as a touchstone and reminder or a *physical representation of whatever magic I'm trying to manifest* so that every time I look at it or hold it, I think of my wish, and the intention continues to build.
The beauty of crystals and rocks is that they are living energies and divine and the thirteenth frequency. They will make your life better just by being near them as they are energy raisers.
I urge you to communicate and get to know these Earth Angels. A real relationship with magical tools takes time to build, but in the end, the crystals will tell you what you should do with them.

Chapter 11
Protection

P lease always do a protection spell or circle of protection for yourself BEFORE you do divine connection work outside the Earth realm, such as soul retrievals, spirit work, communicating with entities, or even divination work.

I understand working with spirits via divination or soul traveling sounds exciting. Some people are drawn to Witchcraft because they like the feeling of aliveness and are exhilarated by fear and the darker aspects of the craft. Whatever excites you is fabulous, but you need to be safe.

Protection of yourself is critical, as is the safety of your home if you are doing spirit work. Please always protect yourself mind body and spirit.

Physically take care when you work with fire energy. Don't leave candles burning when you are not around. Do be aware embers are dangerous bits of fire waiting to take hold. Distinguish your smoke sticks, incense, and candles with care.

I want to get serious with you magical beings right now. Sometimes you need protection against a simple human. Bully issues – no problem a piece of cake to take care or. Perhaps you want to keep your home safe from thieves or bad luck? Easy peasy just grow some Rosemary around your front door, put up a protection altar in your home or hang some Witch balls about and those will do the trick.
That's the easy protection stuff.
But if you work with spirits and divination then you need an entirely different and more powerful protection around you.

I travel between worlds as an Angelic channel I have interacted with many different energies on the other side. Please know that all spirits are not good intentioned.

All spirits are not our friends, and the bad ones are tricksters as well. If you purposely align and work with unknown spirits just for fun, such as asking questions of the Ouija board without instructing WHO you want to help you, you may be calling in forces you really don't want around you. Once you purposely invoke a spirit to aid you in answering a question that is a contract, they helped you and they may expect something in return. Instead of some well- meaning spirit that comes in to help you with your question out of their divine hearts, you could get a cling on spirit that attempts to stick around and use your energy.

I don't want to scare you, but working with spirits is serious magick, and I'd be remiss if I didn't warn you and give you protection to armor yourself when you deal with these unknown spirits.

Candle Protection

Another way to invoke protection is to light a candle and infuse it with what you want protection.

Light the candle and say:

"With this light I protect myself
With the flame and power of the element of fire
So be it."

Invoking a circle for protection

You can use a wand, a smoke stick, or your own finger. Draw an imaginary circle around yourself and say this spell:

"In this circle I am protected
All bad things are reflected
So mote it be."

Visualization Protection

You can always invoke a protection circle around yourself with visualization as well. Sit down, clear your mind and imagine a circle of mirrors around you as you sit peacefully in the center.
On the inside, you are protected and untouchable; on the outside, the mirrors will send back any energy heading your way back to the original source.
In this circle, you are protected. Know it to be so, and it is done.

Sound Protection

One of my favorite magical tools to use for protection is the singing crystal bowls. I have one tuned to the F note, which is the heart chakra. It is perfect for protection because love is the thirteenth frequency and thus divine.

I like to strike the side of the bowl three times with the mallet and then slowly rim the bowl until a sound cone emerges of such strength I feel enveloped in it.
At this point, I declare myself protected by all that is divine, so be it.

As a magical person you may have no religious affiliation, which is fine neither do I. You can choose a goddess or being that you feel is a protective energy for you or do any of the basic protection spells I just gave you that do not need any protector deity associated with it. If you would like to use my prayer and you don't believe in Jesus in a religious sense, you can still call in the *Christ Energy* to protect you.

Jesus is available to the entire human race and will come when you need him. It is the contract he made to us all long ago. The Christ Energy has been impregnated for thousands of years with magic and miracles and it is always available to you and will protect you.

Super Divine Protection Prayer

In the name of Christ Jesus I cast away all low frequency energies in my body, in this room, in this home and neighborhood.
So be it.
In the name of Christ Jesus I call in the divine love frequency in the name of Christ to protect my body, this room, this home and neighborhood.

So be it.

Chapter 12 COVENS AND FRIENDS

C lassic Witchy and wizard conditions like group meditations and belonging to a Coven are fun to do with like-minded friends.

When you imagine the Witches of old, you think of a group of beings dancing around a fire creating magic together, and I say – let's keep this tradition going, Witches!

Although I'm a solitary Witch by nature, I adore groups of good energy Witches or friends when they gather to do magick. A great group of people manifesting together can lift you up and help your wishes come through quickly. Together you can support and pray for each other's wishes and thus power up all of the intentions. Groups always create more energy together if they are all good vibes.

A word of warning when it comes to any new group you may not know. Don't just jump into any group to be a part of something because they want you to join. Magick depends on the energy of the people and your safety is important too.

Please research and check your gut meter to see if a new group of people resonates with what your soul wants and believes.

If you are interested in the power of group manifestations than you can always ask your friends to join you in creating a magical group of conscious intenders (they don't have to be self-proclaimed Witches)

If you have a like-minded group of cool magical friends (high-frequency) and if you add a bonfire (high frequency) and stream or river (high frequency) and moon energy (high frequency)
maybe add some dancing (high frequency) and singing (high frequency) – well, all the wishes you want to manifest will be flowing in quickly I can assure you!

In the end, it's all about getting high frequency.

They always show covens in movies in some scary bad outfits in some weird haunted-looking swamp – HUMPH! I like seaside circle groups myself, and anytime there's a fire I'm bringing marshmallows…

The bottom line is that all those classic Witch-like traditions raise energy up to a high frequency and from there magic appears. Church groups and Covens do the same thing. The group energy united lifts frequencies up to the magical divine level and all good things come in from there, be it prayers or spells.

If you want to wear a cape and howl at the moon then you sound like a heck of a lot of fun to me. I'll bring my Harry Potter wands and let's go make some wishes come true.

Chapter 13

Clairvoyance

Clairvoyance means receiving messages in the form of pictures and or symbols. Nostradamus is famous for his seeing into the future. Edgar Cayce got his visions through dreams.

Do you get pictures or visions? Do you SEE things? If so, then clairvoyance may be your clearest gift.

Even if you have a combination of all three, one is usually stronger. If clairvoyance is your primary gift you will see pictures, movies, or flashes of images that may tell the future or give you special insight.

Sometimes you will understand the vision right away and other times it may seem to make no sense at all.
Don't bother with trying to understand all the images now. Often events come to pass in time and you will recognize that you *saw this already.*

Sometimes you will get pictures that make no sense to you. Once while trying to help a young woman to heal the wound left by her mom's untimely death, I felt like I was failing her

She didn't need to mend her relationship with her deceased mother as so many people do that want to connect with their dead loved ones. She just needed to be sure there was *really an afterlife* and that she could still have her mom near her even if she were on the other side.
(Which, by the way if you're wondering - you always have your deceased loved ones near you while you're still on Earth. Once on the other side you are multi-dimensional and can sustain your spirit in many different places including sticking right next to the people you love best while building a star system in Vega.)

Because I HEAR things (clairaudient), I started hearing her mother. I repeated what I was getting but I wasn't telling Donna anything that made her feel that it was HER mother and not some well-meaning guide or Angel.

It was a late night after a party which is never a good time to do clear work and I suggested we try again another time. Suddenly, I started getting pictures of a beautiful tree with orange and yellow leaves. I was nestled into the branches and marveling at the colors. I had no idea why I had the vision, but the leaves got clearer and clearer of the tree with the autumn colors. I finally turned to her and blurted out,

 "What's up with the FALL?"

She grabbed me and said,"Oh my God, she fell off a mountain into a tree. That's how she died she landed in a tree."

Okay, so first of all what a horrible tragedy my heart went out to her. Second, I was soooo happy that I had helped her connect without me personally seeing anything scary! I have no desire to see graphic violent scenes and so I don't. Yet, I was still quite stunned that a flick of the word could change everything. I said *fall* instead of *autumn, which was in my head.* Somehow spirit had FALL come out of my mouth, which meant nothing to me but *everything to her.*

So note!!! What you get when you communicate with people and spirits on the other side or other dimensions may not make sense to you right away.

Don't judge what you get just share it.
A top psychic friend of mine that read me kept seeing a toilet and I finally said my boyfriend's a plumber! Not life-changing, but she did get what energy was around me.
I flushed him out of my life FYI.

Okay, the second big thing to take away from this personal account is that I didn't see anything horrible. No blood, no death, nothing scary – YET from what occurred Donna now had no doubt her mother had reached across the divide of death to communicate.

I can understand that many people don't want to see scary things, I concur, in that case you can set boundaries. I'll show you how later on.

Chapter 14 CRYSTAL BALL SCRYING

A great way to work on your visions is with a crystal ball. Remember to do a protection ritual or prayer before consorting with the crystal ball as it is a very powerful divination tool and has the ability to bring in spirits.

You can use any crystal if you don't have a crystal ball. When choosing your fist vision ball, I might go for a clear glass ball as large as you can get.

Actual organic crystal balls are better, of course, they have more energy, but they are more expensive as well and a bit harder to start with.

Here are some basics of learning to work with scying. Get into a trance space, through breath or double drumming tapes and ask your query of the ball.

Darken the room your working in and arrange candles near your vision ball. The flames will flicker and cast images off the surface.

Soften your gaze and allow your mind to run free as it watches the flickering of shadows and forms across your ball.

Allow yourself to see what the ball is trying to share.

This is a practice; so don't expect to be an excellent crystal ball reader right off the bat.

In fact, it can be quite draining at first working with scrying so expect that when you begin.

Great success comes with discipline. Keep at it.

Working with scrying will help strengthen your gift of vision. You are building a magical skill that will serve you later. Good job.

Chapter 15 Tarot and Oracle Cards

An excellent way to enhance and work with your clairvoyance is with the Tarot cards.

Tarot and oracle cards are not only a lot of fun to use, but they also help build your psychic power. Even though I know the traditional meanings of the tarot cards, I often throw them out the window during a reading and just let the cards speak to me together.
There are infinite ways to work with magical tools and everything is right!

The Tarot is ripe with imagery, and we can all see different things in a card. If you would like to try and enhance your clairvoyance ability,

I recommend getting a Tarot deck or an oracle deck.
Pick one that appeals to you. There are thousands to choose from including Fairy cards, Mayan Calendar cards, Voodoo cards etc. Pick a deck that the images speak to you.

Make sure you do a clearing or protection spell over the cards before your first use with them and also any time you do a reading for anyone other than yourself.

Now lets just start working with the cards.

It's a great practice to learn the meanings of the cards to have a foundation of the archetypes that have continued throughout the centuries.
After you've gotten to know the meanings of the cards, I advise letting your imagination take you to where the cards want to bring you.
Tarot is a tool that speaks to you visually, and builds a relationship with you. Maybe a particular card always means YES to you no matter what other people believe.

Again, this is a craft and will take time to perfect, but it's also fun and will help strengthen your inner eye and gift of prophecy.

As a note, I personally don't use my cards to predict the future for myself or anyone else.
I use divination systems to tell me what my or another *persons' current energy is creating.* In other words, if they tell me they want something I use the cards to see if it is close or if they need to go in a different direction to achieve their goals.

I don't believe the cards tell you what you are stuck with but what your potential is at that moment. If you don't like a future foretold by the cards – take a left my dear! This is why prophecy is a gift. It helps give you a heads up to reassess and change. You can change your path if you don't like where you are headed, or stay straight onward if you are headed to where you want to go.

I love the Tarot and oracle decks to help me open and strengthen my third eye and my clairvoyance power –
however, I recommend that you DO NOT use Tarot or any divination or oracle system if you're currently manifesting something with Witchcraft and you are waiting for your magical wish to appear!

Divination is for when you *don't know.*

The power behind the manifesting something with a spell is believing that *you do know.*

Do not cross create against your own magic.
Sending out contradictory messages of intention will sabotage your workings.
 NO NO, NO magical beings.

Stay steady. Stay in belief. Stay happy and expect it to show up.
Stop asking the universe if it's going to show up via an oracle deck when you already ordered it!!
Go dance or something will you?
That would be way more helpful in helping pull your wish into the third dimension!

Chapter 16

Clairaudience

Clairaudient people have a developed sense of hearing. They HEAR things, sometimes they hear entire conversations in their head that have taken place. Perhaps they hear spirits on Earth and beyond.

You may hear something, and it just doesn't sound right. What is your gut trying to tell you?
If you get voices and conversations in your head, perhaps people saying things you've already heard before - then you might have the hearing gift of clairaudience.
Oddly it's not just hearing voices in your head; it can be understanding or the clarity of listening to a person or conversation and hearing something that no one else did in the conversation.

The art of authentic listening.
As a note, because this is my personal gift it's amazing to me that often what I consider rather logical seems psychic to others.

I had a client that wrote me many times wanting a session with me. Each time she wrote me, she talked about her love of Florida and the beach and told me how much she yearned to move back there. When we had our session, the first thing she said to me was –
"I want to move. I've asked five different psychics where I should move, and they all said different things. One said Sedona, another Salem, and one said to look for a forest –where do you think I should move?"
I said. "I think you should move to Florida."
She lit up and said, "YES, yes that's it! Florida! You're so talented!"
Ummmm.
Really? Well maybe. Or maybe I just LISTENED.
So dear ones, the art of clairaudience is being able to listen fully. We will build on this talent during the meditation chapters.

Chapter 17

Clairsentience

C lairsentient is the ability to FEEL the truth or that something is going to happen. It is a gut sense of knowing.
If you have a good gut sense, that means you are deciphering information and frequencies through your feeling sense.

I believe that clairsentience is the most common and possibly the most ignored!
You may also hear people that have this enhanced gift as EMPATHS.
They feel you. They are empathetic and they understand your frequency.

Since the beginning of time, we have been relying on our sixth sense gut deciphering of frequencies for our survival. Over time we may not need that knowing sense to avoid attacking wolves or predators, but we still need it to avoid those annoying coworkers.

Honestly, we still use our gut sense to make a bulk of our choices (that aren't ingrained habits.)

So to receive messages in this FEELING way, you might feel a tug in your stomach, or an electrical jolt run through you like a shiver or the hair on your arms stand up. One of the best things you can begin to do is write down and remember all the times when you do FEEL something over the next few days and put it down in your Book of Shadows so you will remember.

Learning to understand how your inner barometer of attunement works and understanding yourself is critical to understanding messages when they come.

Chapter 18
Inner Magic

M agic lives in us both as an inner knowing and outer manifestation ability. The inner knowing, *empathy* and prophetic powers use your ability to *decode frequencies.*
The external use of frequencies involves creating something you desire into your reality. I will refer to this as creating or manifesting with frequency attunement *or Witchcraft.*

The inner magic includes your ability to decode energy and see the future. It is the ability to enter source vibration at will.
being, alien, or entities across all dimensions.
This inner knowing is also referred to as the inner eye or psychic knowing. Your ability to ward off danger by being warned ahead and thus to change your choices when you see or know a path is coming

you don't desire. We are mostly made up of this source of energy so tapping into it is natural.

This inner eye is very deeply rooted and is already encoded in your DNA primary SURVIVAL mode. So, in other words, you're born with this magical ability to predict what's coming and protect yourself.

But what you're really doing is reading a thing's energy or FREQUENCY..

Now – do you consciously use it or know how to use it? Probably not because it is instinctual. Like swallowing. But I will do my best to break it down into bite-size pieces to digest it easily and remember.

Your INNER magic also allows you to access all other spirits/souls across the universe.

The space that we share with the entire universe and all spirits is just that *shared.* It is filled with love, and we are mostly made up of it. Connection and communication are hardwired in you.

Outer Magic

O uter Magic is making things appear like magic.

Oh, so you want something?:)

Then you want to do some outer magic and make something materialize no problem!

Your outer magic is just as natural to you as your inner magic. Manifesting things you want into the *physical world*, is where we move into the yang and material or the outer projection of your abilities into the universe. Producing something out of the ether without money looks like magic because most people don't know how to use their own gifts of creation.

Creation stems from a triangle agreement and an alignment with the frequency of the thing you want to pull into your life. Then you need the power of your wanting desire or love to breathe life into you wish.

Love is the overwhelming constant in things that appear.
The frequencies come FROM YOU and what you LOVE.

Love Magic

Love is the highest energy. It's the space-frequency of 13, and it's what we are made of. If space is genuinely God, then it is filled with love, and thus love is God in action.
Love melts all evil and creates instant magic.
I've seen it myself over and over again and I'm not just saying that because I'm a goody two shoes LA Witch. It's because I've seen love work. Love is miracle energy.
Love creates things, and love is a frequency you can't fake. Everyone knows when someone is in love with an item or person. I'm sure all of you magical people have had the experience of spontaneously manifesting something you love with no tools or maybe thought about it other than you love it. For a concrete down to Earth example of how this magic works naturally and all the time, here's a simple story.

I was at a new friend's home and went to their bathroom. I was enamored with a humorous toilet painting that was hanging on the wall and it made me laugh.
When I came out of the loo, I just gushed about how much I loved the artwork and how I needed to find the artist to buy some of her work.
The hostess looked at her husband, and then she opened a closet, pulled out the *exact same painting, and handed it to me.*
I looked confused, and she said. "We bought two because we love it and wanted to give it to someone else that might love one as well – and that person is you!"
Love got me that picture in less than a minute of my desire coming out of my mouth!

LOVE works that fast.

I channel Aphrodite and many know of her as the angel Goddess of Beauty and love – but let's look at the love part. Love refers to love in all respects not just romantically. In fact the church of Aphrodite is the worship of the act of love in progress. Miracles in action always occur in the love space.

Now onto getting *you what you want* my dear ones – here is my easy beginner *5 Step Spell to Get What You Want.*

Chapter 19 5 Step Spell To Magically Get What You Want

I'm going to teach you a simple spell to help you learn the basics of the science of magic and how to use it to your advantage. Manifesting is making MAGIC APPEAR in reality!!

After multitudes were made aware of the law of attraction by hits like *The Secret,* I noticed a demand for the "How To" part that was never mentioned in the famous work.
People understood and believed in its message; they didn't have any idea how to do it! Just as the mechanics of riding a bike and *riding* the bike are two very different entities.

After I broke the code in the Mayan Calendar and went into the Mayan Rainforest I had a transformative experience, which led to my understanding of the universal science of vibration, which was shown to me in the form of frequency attunement. From this adventure I wrote my first book. ULTIMATE POWER – the understanding of frequency attunement.

After the book was published, I went on to lecture to large audiences every month on the new science of frequencies. With the information I received through my dreams and the research I did in the Rainforest, I developed a way to show other people how to step-by-step create a wish that comes true. In other words – how to do MAGIC.

> To simplify this process, I developed this *five-step magic spell for beginners.*

When we are younger, we tend to manifest things naturally because one of the most potent parts of the process is loving something and having a passion for it. We
have a lot of that as children and less of it as adults. We need to cultivate those childlike moments – they bring you beautiful things and reduce your stress too.

I've talked about building up the love frequency inside you and how it pulls things to you that you want. After you master this step-by-step process and get good at it, then you too will just FEEL the intention, POWER it up with LOVE and let your dream arrow fly. Remember we have been spontaneously creating this way our whole lives. We have the force of creation within us. We are just now going to do it with purpose and intention infused with the joy of something we really want.
The love and joy as cliché as it sounds are thirteenth frequency things that resonate on the level of miracles and magic. Tapping into the space thirteen. I've found that enthusiasm – also a high frequency is a powerhouse of magic when it is present.

One of the things I wanted as a child was to own a restaurant. As a young girl, I was so consumed with it that I decided to open one up when I was six out of my basement in Buffalo, New York.

I made a sign and put it outside on the snow bank in front of our little house and called it the "Blue Suede Shoes Cafe." I had daily customers despite the blizzard-like conditions.

I look back now and wonder what kind of strange people were coming to a six-year-old's restaurant in her basement? But that's another research project. The real focus is that I was building up to a future manifestation with my love and enthusiasm and in this case also acting AS IF.

Unfortunately, I had reluctant landlords, i.e., my parents didn't like me running a restaurant out of our basement with my Barbie Burger Grill and Easy-Bake Oven. One little fire, and they shut down my business, go figure. Although it was short-lived, I put that frequency out there, and years later, that frequency brought me my restaurant today.

After I channeled the book on frequencies and began to apply what I knew on how to manifest, I started manifesting things in my life that were huge and with no money.

I co-owned a wonderful restaurant for years in the Pacific Palisade in California.

Our tiny place was filled with movie stars and famous people everyday. It was by the beach and it couldn't have been a better experience!

That's how I manifested the restaurant that I had always wanted as a child out of pure love and enthusiasm.

I had powered up my love for it until the timing was right and then POOF the restaurant appeared – like magic!

I want to be clear that this happened with none of my own money. I had no money of my own or savings. I was barely making my rent payment when this opportunity arose to purchase the restaurant it came in without needing any money from me at all. I was a single mom at that time and barely had the money for the electric bill, let alone to go investing in a restaurant.

But still it manifested.

Here I am with Martin Mull and Gene Levy. I loved them!!! And of course the legendary Sir Anthony Hopkins!

Remember, if I can do it, you can do it.
People always want to manifest money – but I manifested my dream with NO MONEY.
I didn't know how it was going to come through and you won't know how it's going to come through, but it will come in a beautiful,

fantastic way, and of that, I can assure you.

Remember I told you that LOVE was the source of power that makes things happen? I LOVED my dream into existence, and SO CAN YOU!!!!

So let's begin with step one!

Chapter 20 Spell Step 1

Decide What to Wish For

Y our first step toward manifesting magic and your dream appearing is deciphering what gets you excited and passionate enough to manifest it.

Or – wait for it – things you LOVE.

Figuring out what really makes you happy and what you really want in your heart and spirit might be the most challenging part of the entire process of manifestation. In the Harry Potter books, no Witch pointed her wand and said, "I kind of want the door open. "They pointed their wand and, with great INTENTION and desire, willed the door to open – *Alohamora!*

What is it that you could bring into your life that would genuinely make your spirit and your heart happy?

You're reading this book to get something. Do you want a material thing or a dream or perhaps to believe that magic exists in this world?

I urge you to go after your dreams. Modern magic means BELIEF and commitment to your desires, but first, you have to dream! Little dreams, big dreams, passions, and love
Because people have so much resistance to even finding out what they really love and what would make them happy, I developed this simple exercise to help you.

This would be a good time to pull out your Book of Shadows. If you initially had a difficult time with figuring out your soul dream and intention -try this exercise!

Step 1: Exercise

Figuring Out What You Want

1) Sit down in a quiet place and take three deep breaths, one for the mind, one for the body, one for the spirit.

2) When you are comfortable and relaxed, I want you to imagine:

Imagine...

You were just given $300 million dollars as a

gift. Now check in with your triangle. Ask your mind what it wants to do with $300 million dollars. Ask your body what it wants to do with $300 million dollars.

Now ask your spirit what dream it wants to follow with the freedom allowed by that $300 million dollars?

Now that you have all the money in the world.

What do you want?

You got it? You sure? You love it? All of you…?

Ahh what? What do you mean ALL OF ME?

Chapter 21 The Triangle Check

O h yeah I forgot to mention the *judges*. Before we move onto the next step we have to talk about your inner triangle.
To manifest in the third dimension you need an agreement of all three sides of yourself to create the geometry of form.
Thus before you get your wish, you still have to get by all three first before the spell works and your wish comes true. I think this information gets left out. You see often *what you think you want* – is not what ALL of you really does want. Sometimes we shut out voices we don't want to hear but are trying to communicate with us.

In the *West,* we tend to listen primarily to our minds and not as much to the voices of our bodies or spirit hearts. However what we manifest always depends on an agreement between the three parts that make up our whole.

Very often, you will find some part of your triangle has resistance. Which means a part of you is unsure. Don't fight that. That voice is protecting you and looking out for an integral part of your happiness. If you don't listen – it will block you anyway! As much as you want to leap straight into your dream, sometimes taking single steps toward it is better.
Sometimes a dream takes steps. This is not because you can't manifest significant things. The fact is, change is scary to most humans.

Big leaps mean big changes.

Your life changes when things change. Things change when you change; sometimes jobs, sometimes friends, sometimes marriages. Even when those things that change are for the better, it can still be scary. When you go to manifest something, you need to realize that you're working with three parts of yourself.

Three little judges, if you will; we have our own little Congressional system and balancing act going on, except in our case, it's the *mind, the body, and the spirit.*
Whether you like it or not, you must pay attention to *what each one of them is saying.* You won't manifest anything or pull it into the third dimension without all three parts of yourself agreeing on it. Ultimately you are using six-dimensional geometry to do this so that it can manifest through the triangle and take form on Earth.

All three parts of you have a voice – and a choice – in what you create. You can't ignore any part of you. In my private practice, I have noticed that the most significant problem people face in manifesting wishes too big. *They get in their own way because they don't really want what they're trying to manifest.*

Again, not that you can't magically make something huge appear – it is just the human part of you prefers slow change – again, your choice

In this process, you take what you think you want and run it by the three judges: *mind, body, and spirit to be sure.*
Take a moment to check in with your triangle. How do you feel?
How does your body feel about it?
This is your BODY MESSAGE.
How does your head think about it?
This is your MIND MESSAGE.
And now how does your spirit react about it coming true when you quiet down and ask it? This is your SPIRIT MESSAGE.
Did you feel excited in all three parts of your triangle?
Is there any resistance? Are all three parts of you ready for this thing to appear or come true now?
If you feel reluctance ask yourself some questions and try to pinpoint the truth for yourself, which that wise part of your being is trying to communicate. If you do feel resistance in part of yourself, can you scale down your wish into a smaller step where you feel more comfortable?
Often time one part of us is really gung ho to create something and then the rest of us is not really onboard. Once you understand what your entire being is ready and wanting – THEN the magic appears quickly.
Make sure you record all of this in your Book of Shadows.

Chapter 22 Spell Step 2

Getting into a High Frequency

So how are YOU feeling?
Are you ready to move ahead with your wish? Are you so ready that if it came to you tomorrow, you'd be pleased about it? If you truthfully answer *yes,* then you're ready.

Good, because we are going to go manifest it, and sometimes it happens right away. I very often have seen things manifest within 24 hours.

Then conversely, at other times, it takes a bit longer to manifest because the pieces have to be put into place. (Such as my restaurant.)
But signs will show up quickly to show you that the message has been received.

Step one; you've identified what you wanted and made sure that all three parts of you are in agreement.
We are ready to move on to Step Two in the process of creation.
Get yourself into the highest frequency possible.

Like attracts like.
Good things come in on good vibrations.
To manifest the quickest, stay in the highest frequency possible all the time.

Remember – a high frequency is anytime you're feeling good, like when you hear birds singing or little kids laughing; whenever love is emanating from you, or you're bouncing
off the walls with joy. Remember higher the frequency, the more divine, happy, and good it feels.

The science of frequencies can get complicated, but to simplify things, remember high frequencies make you feel good, so you should always move toward them. Conversely, low frequencies make you feel bad, i.e., sick, gaining weight, losing your job, losing money, or running into mean people.

Low frequencies feel like quicksand, and the best thing you can do for people in this state is to get them out in nature. Nature, trees especially are the highest divine frequency on the planet – Earth Angels if you will – and just lying on the grass or being in nature will naturally lift a person's frequency.

We are looking for the high frequencies. The high frequencies that make you feel good. *It's imperative to launch a high-frequency wish or goal off of another high-frequency vibration.*

This is where traditional Witchcraft can really help. If you light a candle or create a vision board or crystal touchstone you are working with the high energy of nature and you are powering up the frequency.

How you get high frequency is up to you. If you are a cosmic fan then standing under the new moon and letting your wish float out into the night sky and be picked up the mother moon can aid you. A surefire way to power up you joy force is to watch your favorite comedy! You'll be laughing in spite of what else is going on. Sometimes we just aren't that darn happy and we still need to get stuff done.
Super high frequency things like dancing can be too high a frequency if you're not in a good place, but playing with your wand might be just right. The point is the powering up of your frequency is what Witchcraft really helps you do!

You can use nature and your imagination to get your force zinging when you are manifesting something you want. This is a wonderful time to integrate some magic tools to heighten the good energy. You can use candles for instance or make a shaker bottle or vision board.
I love using my singing bowl to help raise my energy. Sound is very powerful and double drumming is an extraordinary vehicle for getting you into a high vibration. If you work with the elements you might want to call them in. Anything that feels good and lifts your power and helps you get high frequency is what we are looking for.

This is part of the practice. You need to learn to power up your force and move your own energy to a high frequency so you can push those waves of magic out into the universe.

Again – don't forget to use the natural windows and high frequency events when you are feeling them.
Always think WISH TIME when you feel amazing.

A few years ago, I was in Big Sur. I was on a big tree swing in front of my friend's cottage. The swing was one of the most extraordinary things I'd ever been on because it swung out over the highway and over the beautiful valley that also overlooked the Pacific

Ocean. Every time I would swing out over the roadway, people driving by would look up and be totally surprised to see me and wave up to me because it looked like I had fallen out of the sky.

This, for some reason, made me ecstatically happy and joyful. The whole child-like hiding then popping through the clouds and surprising people driving on the road was exhilarating!

I know what makes me happy might not make you happy, but I realized at that moment of silly joy:
Hello Linda, this is Make-A-Wish time!
If you remember nothing else from this book, let it be that every time you get in a super happy place, remember it's wish time – send out those wishes, baby!

Chapter 23 Spell Step 3

Make-A-Wish Movie

Now that you've done Step One and you can identify what exactly you want, and you've done Step Two and you find yourself in a Make-a-Wish high frequency,
NOW is the time to use this technique.
Wherever you are, excuse yourself for a moment, or if you're by yourself in a high frequency already, then you are ready to go.
This step involves making up a movie in your head with real players, imagining what everybody would say, what you would be hearing, and more importantly, what you
would be feeling. Some of the things you should be feeling if you're creating the movie realistically are joy, hooray, and OMG, *my wish is coming true right now.*

Your goal is to create such a believable movie inside your head by using as many senses and creativity as possible that you actually start to get excited about it as if
it was real.
You attempt to fake yourself out.

This is well known but never to be underestimated. "ACT AS IF, and then it shall be."

You fake yourself into a feeling by creating a movie exactly as you'd like to see it playing out in your life, to the point that you get excited about the possibility of it, and the truth of it. When you actually feel excited or
happy, your movie has been successful!

Now that you feel that realness of it, try to hold onto that feeling for as long as possible. Attempt to hold the feeling as if it is actually occurring. The science on this says that you need exactly sixteen seconds to send out a frequency wave.

Your goal is to feel that fake feeling of accomplishment and getting what you want for sixteen seconds or more...

As you're creating this movie inside you, what you're doing is creating a vibrational pattern to send out to the universe that you want *to match* (I.e., the law of
attraction, the law of affinity, like attracts like) so in this movie, you need to use all parts of yourself. It's vital that you use all five senses to roll this movie in your mind.
Imagine it in the *PRESENT* tense: what exactly you want to happen. Imagine what it would look like if this little miracle, this wish. Were coming true, and it was taking place in your life right now.

Most likely, the scenario you're creating is going to have other players and it will probably involve people saying things to you like, "Congratulations you finally got the promotion!" or "That wonderful that girl is on the phone for you…" or even "There's somebody at the door who wants to talk to you about giving you that school grant."

It's going to be a fake movie you make up; only it's the movie you want to see take place in your life.
In the *PRESENT*.
I like to get in a private place and close my eyes, imagining it just like a Hollywood blockbuster.
The most important part of the whole movie is the feeling that it creates in you. What you're feeling in your gut is the frequency-maker that drives your manifestation and pulls in your wish.
Feeling joy for something is the *most crucial* part: it's how we create things.

In this case, you are creating a fake feeling that will send out vibrations to pull in the real thing. It is the art of believing as if it already happened. Some people will call this faith.

Once you are getting to the feeling place and feeling good and excited, you will start to feel it slowly dissipate. The fakeness will begin to show its ugly head. That's perfectly okay. That's normal. Since we know that one of the keys to manifesting is how much energy, i.e., how much feeling, that we put into feeling *as if* it'd just happened, we can conclude logically that the longer we can keep the feelings going, the more likely it appears. And that leads us directly to Step Four.

Chapter 24 Spell Step 4

Keep that Loving Feeling

We have already identified the fact that the longer you keep a feeling going, the more power you put behind it. Those frequencies being sent out are going to find the matching frequencies, i.e., the stronger the frequency output, and the stronger the attraction quality.

The next step involves keeping the feeling going. We need to keep the feelings from the movie that you made in your head, albeit the fake movie, revved up and powerful. As I mentioned, it takes at least sixteen seconds to form a vibrational wave pattern.
The longer we can keep that pattern generating, the quicker it will manifest in your life.

To keep these fake feelings motoring up, we're going to use a little trick I came up with to extend the feeling so you have a stronger vibrational push.
This trick involves bringing in people that you love that will be happy for you if your wish comes true.

Jesus mentions when two or more pray together that miracles happen because the divine force joins them. I guess it's the Holy Trinity coming true, but once again we
are dealing with the triangle. Consequently, if you imagine that you're telling somebody who really loves you that your wish came true, and they connect to you in your wish, then you will enact the divine force of the Trinity, and it will join into creating your desire. The way you're going to use this is right after you accomplish Step Three and create the movie in your head.

The movie gets you into the feeling of, "Wow, this is awesome, this is what it would be like if it were truly taking place."
The *goal is to hold that fake feeling as if, for as long as possible, at least sixteen seconds.*

As we know, this feeling will begin to dissipate, and when it does fade, this is when you *imagine* telling the story to somebody that you care about who would be happy for you.
Retell the story, and more importantly, relive the happy feelings and *feel* them. You make the sensations real again for you, (remember, fake it before you make it!). Like attracts like – use that law of affinity!

For example, you might imagine telling your mother some great news – you got the promotion you were hoping for, you got the grant you were applying for, you got the date that you'd been dreaming of...imagine telling your mother or your close friend and envision how happy they will be for you!

While you are conjuring this, the feelings of their joy will combine with the feelings of *your* joy and rev up those feelings again, which will create more frequencies. Whoopee! Try and keep it going for sixteen seconds!

At this point, throw in another good friend! Tell it to them too! Tell it to Grandma! Tell it to everyone.

"I'm so proud of you!"

"I'm so happy for you!"

And you? You'll say, "I'm happy too! I can't believe how lucky I am. This is the greatest day of my life."

Bingo.

You're smack in the middle of creating those feeling frequencies that are flowing out into the universe to get you those feelings for real. To get you what you want for real. All that joy and success for real, the ability to tell that story for real, to the same real people someday.

This is what creating your life with intention is all about.

This is what it is like to live a truly magical life.

Do not just go every day into what is dealt you like somebody on autopilot. Create your life; make it happen the way you want it to happen. I know you can do it.

Chapter 25 Spell Step 5

Let Go

Okay, we are rounding the bend to the last step and this truly is going to be the easiest.

To recap:
Step 1 – We figured out what we really want.
Step 2 – We've gotten ourselves into a high frequency.
Step 3 – We have imagined a movie in our head that made it feel real.
Step 4 – We extended those fake feelings by pretending to tell somebody we care about. We've reached the final step.

Step 5 - Letting go with gratitude.

So here we are, at the end, and you're about to manifest what you want. The last step involves letting go and being grateful.

It's very important to realize that things come in on frequency levels, so your only job from here on out is to stay away from any thoughts of worry that your
Manifestation might not come true.

This is where it gets a bit tricky and you're going to have to really go with your gut on the truth of this. If you're really just loved, jazzed, and passionate about something but not *worried*, then that's the best place to be. If you feel really good but just haven't seen anything show up, it is okay to quickly redo the exercises I just gave you.

If you're freaking out and afraid and think it's not working, then it's not working. Worry is a low-frequency. You need to let go. Be cool with a divine, nonchalance that it is arriving in perfect time and stay in a grateful place *as if* it's already arrived.

Stay in a high-frequency.

Your job is to get out of any low-frequency of fear and find a way back up into the high-frequency of faith. Which comes down to letting it go, and letting it come in, and being thankful for it *as if* it had already
happened.

Often when people really want something, they can't help but be concerned that it might not come in. Yet this
is the leap you have to take. It's called a leap of faith. You have to let it go.

I think one of the most important parts of this step is being grateful and thankful. I often thank my Angels and guides for the things that I haven't seen show up in my life yet, as well as for the things that have shown up in my life. In this way I keep saying, "I have faith, you're bringing it in. I'm already grateful."

Appreciation. It's a good thing. It helps being grateful. Not to mention being grateful is a very high-frequency!

Okay so you said thank you to the universe for sending it to you and released it into the hands of the divine. You've done everything you could do, including remembering to maintain a high-frequency.

Some ways to accomplish raising your frequency are to go out in nature, dance, play with pets, and continue to do things that make you happy and bring you
up to a good high-frequency feeling place. The high frequencies always magnetize things to you quicker.

   A common question I get in my lectures is "...How long do I have to wait before my wish shows up?"

As I said before, when you get very clear and you really love something, and you don't have fear around it, and you're enthusiastic about it, then it can show up immediately. I've seen things show up within 24 hours – sometime sooner.

Conversely, sometimes you have to wait for the divine order of things to fall into place.
Sometimes certain things in the universe – or people – have to be moved around and put into position for your wish to manifest, and that can take time. Especially if it involves other people – then you also have to deal with the timing of them.

Keys to Supercharge Your Magic

This is the perfect time to integrate fun Witchy and spiritual practices to keep the fire glowing if you will.
If what you want isn't manifesting right away. It just may be the timing is not right. I know it sounds cliché, but the universe works

that way too.

In the meantime why not have some fun with it? Remember wishes come in and MAGIC WORKS only in the high frequencies. So can you integrate more fun and play around this wish until it appears?

"Even the least among you can do what I have done and even greater things."
　　　　　　Jesus

Chapter 26 Spells/Affirmations

While we are joyfully expecting our magical wish to appear, this is the perfect time to do some LIGHT-HEARTED daily spells and affirmations.

I have a list of YouTube videos I recommend to my clients to help repattern their destructive patterns of self-worth from childhood that are very, very helpful. Sometimes it is not that the wish you want is not appearing; it's that you are blocking it with your false belief system ingrained so deeply you didn't know it was there.

Some of these lack of worth issues are planted very early and held at a level you are not aware of. Thus the mass affirmations in effect rewrite over your old beliefs until they are your NEW beliefs. All you have to do is listen.

I'm not a big fan of saying MASS affirmations – again, I'm the Lazy Witch but listening to mass affirmations in the background or walking is very beneficial.

Look, if you haven't noticed, I'm a firm believer in that if it's not fun, there is no magic happening. If you are pushing yourself to do anything, just stop now. The universe heard your wish; it is coming. Maybe you need to just work on faith?

I'm just adding these extra's to do if you're needing support and wanting to do more –
I recommend you play more than with your wish.
This is a great time to create a spell for yourself to symbolize your wish. Remember, it is your practice; you can't get it wrong. Make up a spell with words or actions and use your imagination. Fun powers up your force, and a strong force means strong manifesting. It's the intention that creates and your passion or force that brings it in.

I am a channel for a few ascended master angels, and I only work with divine loved filled spirits. I have also found the highest magical beings are also the most fun to hang out with!! The divine beings I've connected with are really goofy and fun and not at all serious as I imagined.
This is why I say play with your spells; it is supposed to be fun and powerful. Oddly they travel together!
The bottom line again is – do you!! You can't go wrong. If you want serious, do serious – do you.

If you want to write your own spell, it is very easy, and there are no rules. You can make your spells long or short, but I like a few lines, and rhyming creates a magical cadence that seems to add some oomph. Again I'm a Lazy Witch, so I generally keep my intention magic simple, easy, and light.

Here's an example of a spell or affirmation I wrote while I was manifesting world travel.

"Twiddle dee dee

> Look at me
> The world travel I desired
> I do now see
> Yippee!"

The point is that the words take on power because you repeat them in the present expecting tense as if it's already happened -and it's fun.

Key take away –
ACT AS IF IT HAS ALREADY OCCURRED.

Have fun and stay as high frequency as possible.
Remember, you want to stay away from doubt. So if you're hovering over a black candle all day muttering serious spells while you worry, doubt, and fret – *nothing is going to happen.* Whether you feel like it or not, whether you are desperate or not, you have to act confident that your magic is working.

If you need money badly, and many people do – remember to stay focused on WHY YOU WANT MONEY. So say you want money to save your home, you could write an affirmation like this -

> "Money money comes to me
> I adore you, baby can't you see
> My bank account is overflowing
> Abundance everywhere I'm going
> So mote it be."

I have noticed seen people throw up blocks to money – old patterns I'm sure, so what might be better would be to word your affirmation spell to get money to save your home like this:

> "My home is protected,
> safe and sound
> All is well,
> and love abounds.
> So be it!

This is a much more potent prayer/ spell.
This DEMANDS protection from everything – including loss of home and does not bring up any lack of money issues you may have.

What it doesn't do is show weakness.
It shows faith, which is strong magic indeed.
But hey, if you can do a happy call out to money spell without being desperate - do it!! Money is an energy, and it is drawn to nonchalance and confident frequencies, so play with it!!!!

Where's my Darn Wish?

I would suggest as a hint, if you do not see your manifestation come through right away, to retry the whole five steps when in a high-frequency.

Run through the process again and send it out again. Not in a stressful, fearful way, but just when you identify a high-frequency moment. Send out another mini version of the wish. The other thing I would do is go back and recheck and make sure that you're not wishing for something too big a step *for you* (according to your triangle).

Re-examine and see if there is any part of the wish that you are having a bit of resistance to. If yes, perhaps you can start with trying to manifest a slightly smaller step.

I know you can do it!

Chapter 27
Glamour Spell

Being able to enchant others with your looks and or beauty is a powerful charm for certain. Kings have given up their kingdoms to win the love of beauties. They still do. In my opinion, having great beauty is more powerful than having lots of money.

Beauty is a thirteen frequency that all beings respond to – Hail to Aphrodite.
If you want to power up your attractiveness with a *Glamour Spell* forever or just a day, then do this.

1. *Pray to Aphrodite*. She's the Goddess of beauty. If you really want to be attractive for eternity and not just a moment, I suggest you learn to attune to her frequency and appreciate the gifts she brings. I keep a lovely statue of her on my altar to keep her close all the time.

2. *Believe you're beautiful or handsome even if you aren't*. My magical grandmother, who was a legendary beauty until she died at

96, used to say to me repeatedly when I was young (and, as I mentioned, very unattractive.)
"If you just believe you're beautiful, everyone else will too."
As a child who was bullied for my ugliness, I clung to this phrase like a life preserver. It became my personal spell that I repeated over and over to myself for many years until I believed it.

3. *Shine your light out with confidence.* Imagine your energy boldly pushing and shining out from you like you are the Sun casting rays of golden light outward. Hold your head high and meet people's eyes and smile widely for no reason.

4. *Do everything physically possible to help your looks.* Back in the day, I checked out 50's beauty books on how to condition your hair, so it shone and walk with better posture.
In our modern-day, you can log onto YouTube and learn anything you want about beautifying yourself. The world of beauty is at your fingertips via your computer. Go dive in and learn all the tricks you can to make yourself as attractive as possible.

We live in a 3-D world where things are made real through the geometry of the triangle taking form and materializing it.
This triangle is enacted when your mind, your spirit, and your body are all involved in creating your wish. Thus the wishing, the wanting, and the doing must all come into play to make a spell work.

I will add that confidence is a hallmark of power – and beauty. If all else fails, fake it till you make it, baby.

Sometimes you will need to pull the Glamour out when you're not ready or prepared physically, and that's going to take *confidence* to pull off. One day I unexpectedly ended up at a fancy restaurant for lunch, and I was wearing a t-shirt and grey sweatpants just having come from a workout. I had no time to go home and change. I had to deal. So I pulled my Glamour on.

I took out my ponytail and fluffed my hair as best I could. I rolled up my sweatpants above my knees and put on some old high heels I found in the trunk. I took a deep breath and sauntered into that swanky place in my workout gear like I was walking up the red carpet at the Golden Globes.

I thought I was pulling it off, too - until the hostess chased after me as I was on my way to the powder room.
My heart lurched.
Good grief, was she going to tell me I wasn't dressed appropriately? (Which I wasn't!)
Nope.
She looked at my sweatpants and gushed,

"Girl, I love your pants! Where can I get some?"

(Insert eyebrow raise here.)

The moral is:
Fake it with confidence and know your Glamour Spell is working as long as you believe it!

Chapter 28

Invisibility Cloak

Being able to disappear easily or walk about unnoticed is a very useful ability to have.
Sometimes we just don't want to be seen.
Other times there is negative energy about, and you don't want to stick out as a target.

This is akin to the Glamour Spell in that your belief is the most essential aspect of the spell being successful.

In the Glamour Spell, you're emanating out beauty and confidence. When you want to be invisible, you want to *close and suck in your energy.*
First of all, if you feel any energy is *dangerous,* even if you don't know why – protect yourself first!

Get away from the dark energy as quickly as possible!!!

Your first course of action then is to disappear literally. Get out of there and don't be a looky-loo trying to figure out what some nasty fuss is about. Live to read about it in the papers the next day – don't stick around – *disappear!*

Then there are times when you just don't want to stick out nor be seen for whatever reasons. You're in a bad mood, or you're stuck in a large group, etc., and darn Harry won't lend you his Invisibility Cloak. So conjure up your own. Accio Invisibility Cloak, please!

Invisibility Cloak Spell

1. *Imagine your energy pulling in closer and closer to your body.* Take a deep breath and imagine you are sucking in your energy field around you like another skin. Pull all your energy close around you and imagine it shielding you and becoming darker in color.

2. *Hide yourself physically as much as possible.* If you have a coat on, draw it over you and up to your neck. If you have a hat, put it on and or pull it down further on your head. You can also use your hair to cover your face on each side. Physically make yourself smaller in your mind. Do not stand up straight and keep your head down.

3. *Keep your eyes straight ahead, and don't make eye contact with any person.* Move quickly and with purpose but don't run or make sudden moves to stick out. Keep your hands by your side or in your pockets.

4. *Feel closed off and invisible.* Act as if you can't be seen.

This spell works great all the time, and I use it often! I hope you find value in it.

Chapter 29 CHARLATONS

I've known quite a few charlatan Witches in my years. Southern California is full of so-called Witches that specialize in the darker side of magic that they are so willing to do for *a price.*

In this dimension, all frequencies are mathematical, so what you put in, you will get out. Thus throughout this book, I will steer you away from the darker arts of jinxing, hexing, and cursing for your own good. Of course, if you like the darker arts and that is what brings you joy - go for it.

Since I am offering my personal experiences working with magic, I'll just steer you over to success magic instead of revenge because success is soooo much sweeter.

Just as in real life, somehow, the darker news and darker side of magic have an allure. An associate of mine that works with the darker aspects of Witchcraft makes all of her money off of the fear of

her clients. She scares them, and then she offers to fix the curses that she tells them they are under.
Sometimes she casts a spell that will hurt someone.
Big money in that, sadly.
This charlatan drives a new Mercedes, she lives in a huge beach house, and she looks like a hag!
I mean it!! Despite all the things her cursed money has brought her, she can't outrun the energy she creates – and neither can you.
It lives in you.
Therefore she barters in the dark arts, and her vibration is yucky. She looks sucked in and has wrinkles even Botox can't help. She's never had a boyfriend or lover in the thirty years I've known her.

Her choice to barter in the low frequencies shows not only in her outer appearance, but she also has a bad vibe and not many friends. You can't escape what you create.
Dorian Gray was a great metaphor of the spiritual truth showing up in the physical.

Let's imagine you eat healthy living natural food – that shows up as healthy and vibrant skin. Conversely, let's say you eat Fritos everyday with six coca colas – well, that will show up in your body and energy as well. Why do people GLOW – it's not just the physicalness of being attractive it's the beauty of the soul and spirit that makes one glow from the inside out.

So back to the haggard dark art Witch, I happen to know…
Her ugly energy she barters with shows,
in her energy and her appearance.
She looks haggard.
She looks like a HAG?
Perhaps not a coincidence that Witches have been referred to as such???

Glinda the Good Witch always looking twinkly beautiful. I'll take that, thank you!

I know many Witches are not judgmental of others Witches practices, but I care about you. So while I will not judge – I will lovingly warn you, dear magical being, that the bad stuff you put out can and will boomerang on you!

You can't escape this because, scientifically, things appear if the frequency is matched.
Low frequencies bring more low frequencies – and in the realm of low frequencies, your own powers become limited. It's as if you fall into quicksand and lose yourself, so my dear magical beings, whatever you don't CURSE YOURSELF.

Chapter 30 I need a Hex or a Jinx Spell

So you've been hurt.
I'm sorry.
First, if it's still going on, you need to protect yourself because chances are you've let your guard and or frequency level down. If you feel like your life has hit rock bottom and you're just spiraling down, then do these steps to stop bad energy from coming your way.

#1 Get away from the destructive energy as quickly as possible. Limit any future interaction as much as possible with the person or thing that makes you feel bad

2 Do a protection spell and a clearing spell. If the energy is really bad then get in the bathtub or shower and let the Water Angel cleanse your body and aura. Imagine the water as a protective

loving shield around you. Follow this up with a clearing spell with candle, smoke or word.

#3 Cut all ties on social media.

#4 Cut all invisible spiritual cords.

Easy Cord Cutting Spell'

If you've got a real bugger on your hands then let's make sure that their bad energy is cut away from you. One way to do this is with a Cord Cutting Ceremony.
You can do the cord cutting symbolically while you are in the bath or shower or stream or ocean.
Imagine your body and see if in your mind's eye if you see any cords that seem to be connected to you if you don't see anything that is fine too.

Now imagine a huge loving divine hand coming in and ripping the cords out of you.
ROOTS and all.
Some people like to envision a knife cutting through the cords but I like to get that rotten stuff all the way out root and stem - so I rip those suckers out.

Another way to do a Cord Cutting Ceremony is in your magical space. If you own an Athame than this is the perfect time to use it.

Hold your Athame, knife or wand in front of you. Spin in a circle three times holding the tool and imagine you are severing any cord attachments to you.

Say this:

I cut all cords and energy unwanted

> I declare I am free and clear
> No bad energy can connect to me
> I am protected far and near.
> So be it.

If you have been dealing with an enemy than you may have fallen into a low frequency.

Some hallmarks to know you *are low in frequency are gaining weight, losing money or getting a ticket, and feeling confused.* Feeling confused is a huge warning that you are hanging in low frequency realms.

When you are confused, your power is scattered because power is fueled by clarity and clear intention.

If you still need extra protection then lets do a Binding Spell to stop them from using any ill power towards you.

Binding Spell

So we got a jerk on our hands and its going to require more than just getting out of their way. When you have a nasty truly bad person after you then do a *Binding Spell* to stop them from doing harm to you.

If you're dealing with an enemy, it is always good to do some extra protection workings as well.

When I feel I the need to go on the defense, I usually use both my Super Protective Prayer and a visualization of protective energy around me coupled with a smoke clearing.

If I still feel the yucky energy around me or the jerk is just not letting off their attacks on me than it is time to bind them and bury them just to make sure the idiot doesn't surface again.

Before we consider revenge let's stop them. Even if we want to send them bad energy the best thing we can do for our own good is to put a stop to their nastiness toward us now and think about payback later.

Begin the spell by writing the bullies name on a piece of paper and then wrap the paper with twine or string and then put the bundle under the biggest rock you can find to hold it down. If possible take choose a rock far from where you live.

Then say this spell:

"I bind your evil here and now
No more bad can be done no how
Bound and buried all evil is gone
I'm protected from you all life long
So mote it be."

Put the rock on top of the bundle and clap your hands with joy three times.

We've cut ourselves off from the evil person.
We've protected and cleared ourselves from the bad vibration.
We've cut cords and even bound and buried the awful person's power.
That said, sometimes you just need to make sure someone gets their just desserts and we're not talking apple pie sweet now.

We're talking stone cold revenge.

Let's do it.

Chapter 31 I NEED REVENGE

L et's talk about the fact that in real life, sometimes people do horrible things to us. Sometimes it's a co-worker or neighbor or lover, and you want them to get their due.

Do not wrong, but take no shit.

I told you why not to use dark vibrational magic because it hurts you too – so then how do you balance the scales when you've been wronged?

Ahh, my friends, well rest assured the JUSTICE card is symbolic of the math of Karma and she is more than happy to aid you in your quest for revenge. Let me be clear we can make math work for us!!!!

In truth I'm speaking from experience. I haven't always been a sweet little love pie. I've messed up with my bad intentions. I've scared people horribly with my magic and I've hurt them too. Before I understood how strong my force created things, I was like an out-of-control tornado, and even though I never cursed anyone on purpose or with some dark ritual, I sure sent out those bad intentions to the point that I created havoc for others and myself.

I won't go into all my stories but rest assured I realized I needed to put my own revenge feelings in check when a nasty co-worker wouldn't come to work one day because she told the boss I beat the heck out of her in a dream. Remember, you can do things with strong emotion and intention without official magical workings. Intense energy creates quickly.
Power is power, so hold on to yours and don't create unknowingly. Although sometimes some astral kicking butt feels good.

And other times you need REAL REVENGE.

You want payback equal to what was done to you. I totally understand so let's go get that jerk that was horrible to you!

It's Curse Time!

Let's face it. There are nasty people out there and you can suddenly be the victim of their evilness.
They deserve payback.
I agree.
In the physical world you could start a rumor that's untrue,
call their boss and tell them some evil lie and get them fired,
or put sugar in their gas tanks and kill their car.
Now do I recommend those?
NO way Witchy poo!
There is just too much boomerang payback in the physical world.
You could get shunned for the gossip and found to be a liar by all

your friends. You could get arrested for ruining someone's car. You could go to court for harassment for getting someone unjustly fired. Yeah there's payback in the real world.
But there is also payback in the magical world.
I know some people deserve warts on their faces for what they did to you but you don't want to grow one on your face right? I'm going to guess NO!
Because warts on the face never looks appealing on anyone.

But wait – the bad guy deserves some kind of payback right?
I agree.
I'm not going to leave you hanging.
(Little Witch pun there sorry.)

I have the best Revenge Spell EVER that also protects you from any bad throwback or warts!

Do not wrong but take no shit!

Just so you know this CURSE REALLY WORKS I'm going to share a really embarrassing story. (Embarrassing for the jerk that did me wrong I should say!)

Thor.
Oh he was beautiful and tanned and a professional surfer. I thought I was in love. He was an ass. He screwed me over big time and screwed a bunch of other women I'm pretty sure. In any case he broke my heart and betrayed me and even robbed me!!! I was brokenhearted and devastated.
As I mentioned - I had seen how my random anger could create things and I didn't want the Karma of hurting Thor unintentionally although HE DESERVED IT.

So this is where I learned a very good lesson and spell to help me feel okay about staying out of the revenge business.

Oh hail to the Goddess of Karma!

Please believe me when I say -.
Karma is WAY MORE EVIL than you could ever think of being!
Of all the things I imagined should happen to Thor as payback for how evil he was to sweet little old me, I had no idea what Karma had in store for him and this is why the curse I've about to share with you is the best ever.
You stay protected.
And the big jerk gets a wholloping you could never imagine.

Say the following words and substitute the name of the person you want revenge on where I put *jerk* as a name holder and he or she where appropriate.

The ULTIMATE CURSE

"Dear God/Goddess of Karma this person _jerk_____
has hurt me bad.
We both know____jerk____has been horrible to me.
I promise that I won't do anything to revenge this myself,
BUT when you balance the scales and___jerk___has
to pay for his/her treatment of me, my only request is
That you let me know
That the debt has been paid and Karma has been
served to___jerk___for what he/she did to me.

And you let it go.

Then look out bad guy!

Now I can't speak for anyone but myself but let me tell you what happened to that cheating horrible surfer playboy Thor that deserved a curse if anyone ever did.
And I could have done it too – that and six generations down (add cackle here.)

So here's the true story of how this curse worked and Karma got that jerk!!

After the cheating, lying, stealing Thor left me heartbroken and disillusioned, the pain and deception still burned bright, and I was having a tough time trusting again and moving on.
It was a full moon – and I don't have to tell you Witches how that gets your feelings rising. It was about six months after I had worked the spell with the Goddess of Karma.
Being a full moon and being alone, I felt melancholy and broke down and decided I just had to call Thor and speak with him. I hated myself for being weak but I rang him up anyway.

Here is how that conversation went with that jerk verbatim…

"Hey Thor how are you I was thinking about you?"

"Oh how am I Linda? Well let's see – interesting you would happen to call me now when I'm sitting in the emergency room at the hospital."

"Oh wow that's horrible what happened?" I asked innocently.

"Well a few months after we broke up I started to grow a large weird tumor on my penis. The doctors had no idea what it was or how to stop it from growing. I finally got so desperate that when I had my tooth filled today I stole a syringe of Novocain from the dentist's office and when I got home I injected my penis with it and tried to dig out the big tumor myself with kitchen scissors – it didn't go well and that's why I'm in the emergency room…"

Okay.
Deep breath.….Seriously!?????
As much as I had wished this total ass got his due, I never would have thought he'd get it that bad!!
The man injected himself with Novocain and stabbed his own genitals?????
I don't know any curses to make that kind of nastiness happen!!!

Moral of the story –

Let Karma get the jerks!

Karma is waaaaay worse than any hex or curse you can conjure up.

Step back and trust.

Don't dirty your vibration with revenge frequencies.

Focus your beautiful amazing magical energy on happiness and success and than smile down from the mountain of joy and just wave down at that loser with the bump on his penis.

Could You Be Cursed?

If a person is a love-filled powerful person, you can't touch them with a curse. High frequency is like a divine bubble of protection. The low energy or a curse can't match the high energy, and nothing will happen to the would-be victim.
If we use science we can avoid the low frequencies, which pull in more low frequencies. You don't want to be there.
Low frequencies pull in similar frequencies on the same wavelength. So say you lose your job- darn okay low-frequency event – but now you get super depressed – more low frequencies than you perhaps yell at your boyfriend, and he's had enough and leaves you. Maybe you get blind-eyed drunk to get over all this horrible stuff, and when you're driving home, then you get in an accident or jail for a DUI.

Ouch! Low frequency spiraling out of control. So who cursed whom?

One low frequency will pull in another low frequency just like it. These are an example of magnetics and low frequencies groupings that you can control.
You are not under a curse.
You are enveloped in a low frequency spiral.
You can control and stop the bad events by manipulating your energy into a higher loving frequency.

No high-frequency Witch ever got hanged or burned!

It's impossible because the frequency doesn't match!!!
(That said we all have bad days so see my Portal-Jumping Spell if needed.)

For those of you that feel cursed, possibly consider Newton's law of motion.
Things in motion tend to stay in motion.

Things at rest tend to stay at rest.
Things moving in one direction tend to continue in that direction.

So if you are sending out nasty frequencies to someone, you are lowering your own frequency and starting a downward spiral of energy that will draw in more bad energy events. This will look like a curse but by allowing or creating those nasty vibes you're actually the one cursing yourself.

I've never been afraid of a curse—Fie on curses. Nothing bad can touch me because I keep myself on a frequency that does not match the frequency of evil and so can you. Sure we all fall into the slumpy vibrations sometimes but if you are disciplined about keeping your energy high then your natural key note frequency will hover around a 9 or 10 and you can bounce back to your good vibing self easily. If someone tells you they can lift a curse off you, I say BULL! You are the only one who can lift yourself up to the loving frequencies, and you have your heart energy to aid you, which is stronger than any dark magic!!!! They are trying to scare you, and they demean your own abilities.
I've had bad boyfriends get me fired or hurt my cat, and they had no curses involved. Remember, evil can be done with human actions just as simply as a curse but only if the person is on the level that they meet up with that energy.

I fully recommend hanging up in the high frequencies with the cool cats and mighty beings. Come on up, Witches, it's better in the penthouse!

Chapter 32 Portal Jumping

O kay this is by no means a beginner spell but my dear Witch when you need to go you just need to go. This is most likely for a select few of you advanced Witches as it is a rarely needed spell, but if your life is threatened it may be the only way out other than death. Since it is a life or death circumstance all the energy in your body will already be turned on and ready to spiral up to aid you. Survival mode creates a powerful frequency that you can't fake nor replicate so this won't work unless you really need it.

WARNING! *This portal should only be conjured up when your life depends on it as you may leap hundreds of years ahead.*

But – better than burning. (Add cackle here.)

Close your eyes, take three deep breathes and blow HARD as if you are blowing an invisible bubble.

Portal Opening Spell

Portal portal open now
Only I do you allow
With love and light begin anew
Divinely protected I now pass through

When the portal opens in front of you jump in quick.

See you on the other side Witches!

Chapter 33
Cleansing

C leansing is a natural part of your day and should be part of your magical workings as well.

Cleansing refers to clearing the energy that an object, person or a room has. Sometimes the clearing needs to be done on you especially after spirit interaction.

We choose to do this because all things are made of energy and hold energy and we want to keep everything clear of energy we didn't intend and instead bless and cleanse items we work with or areas we work in.

This cleanse is mostly powerful due to your intention.

If I am dealing with intense, scary or strange energy that I am not familiar with I always use this spell/prayer and invoke the highest

energy I connect with which for me is the Christ energy.
When I cleanse energy in a room or thing I always invoke the Christ energy to clear all old low frequencies and then to fill the space with clean pure divine love energy by calling in the Golden Christ energy.

INVOKING PROTECTION CLEANSE

I mentioned this in my working with spirits and ghosts section but will repeat the simple but most powerful prayer/spell here. If you don't relate to Christ in a biblical form perhaps you will try and work with the pure Christ energy of miracles that lives in the impregnation of the word over thousands of years.

If you have a guide, Angel and deity that you relate to more than Christ and feel will protect you than feel free to substitute what or who works for you. You can also invoke the "Loving Universe" or the "Power of Love Energy" if you don't work with guides or deities.

Super Protection Spell to Banish Unwanted Spirits

"In the name of Christ Jesus I demand all low frequencies and energy leave my body, this room, this home and this neighborhood, In the name of Christ Jesus I call in the divine energy of Christ to fill my body with the highest frequency, and my room, my home and neighborhood.
So be it."

CLEANSING WITH SMOKE STICKS AND INCENSE OR CANDLES
In this way we use the power of the herb/ fire to power up your intention of clearing energy.

If you have a cauldron than a smoke stick made of sage is my first choice. Smoke sticks flicker and leave burning ashes so if you don't have a cauldron to accompany you with the flaming stick than perhaps choose incense or a candle.

Remember we're protecting ourselves so we don't need any random fire mistakes. Protection first my dear Witches!!!

Walk through your home and bless it with pure energy. Swirl the smoke around yourself and declare yourself cleared. Swirl the smoke around any object you want cleared and demand it be so.

Clearing Spell for Home or Objects

Walk with your smoke stick and cauldron around the house and demand the area or thing you are clearing be CLEARED. You can add your own spell here something simple might be.

" I clean and protect with smoke and air
This home and objects are now clear
So mote it be."

You can also do this holding a candle or incense.

Clearing Yourself

Perhaps the most important ritual you can do when practicing Witchcraft is to make sure you CLEAR YOURSELF.

I will offer my personal process for this. When I have connected with huge groups of entities needing help very often I am filled with energy to the point that I am shaking.

If you find yourself overwhelmed with extra energy in your body I have found that clapping my hands, stomping my bare feet on the ground and TONING is what works for me to clear my body of excess and unwanted energies— I like to use the HEART NOTE which is the AHHHHHHH vowel but if you are dealing with ancient energy you may find other lower chakra tones wanting to move through and out of you so it may sound more like groaning or a deep OOOOOOOH.

Using a smoke stick is also a wonderful way to cleanse yourself. Simply light the stick and waft it in circular motions around yourself holding your cauldron near it to catch and embers. Imagine yourself cleared and cleansed with the smoke and so it is.

Baths and showers or swimming in a natural body of water is a must for me after dealing with powerful energy and just as a way to clear myself and return to my own energy.

Simply take a bath and release and balance your energy into the Angel of Water, which will clear and protect you. I will often put in certain crystals that are my closest personal stones and put them in the bath with me.

If you are in the bath and or shower or lake etc. And still feeling overwhelmed with energy I recommend to keep using the vowel sounds to move the energy out. Don't think about it just TONE or sing whatever sound wants out of you until you feel you're done.

Before you get out of the bath or shower *proclaim yourself cleansed so be it.*

Remember you are the vehicle that moves the energy that makes universes. You can do anything with just intention. Declare yourself clear and you are.

Chapter 34
Expanding Your Power

W hy are some people capable of pulling in magic into their lives seemingly at will and others are struggling despite doing all the ceremonies or traditional workings of Witchcraft?

If the ceremonial part worked alone we would hear much more success stories of finding true love, health or material things.

Then again, after working with the science part – I know many people who struggled to raise their energy to the point of attracting what they want.

> The art and science of magic can work alone if you're a very powerful force - but they are meant to work together to ensure success!

So why are some magical people successful at creating magic and getting what they want and others struggle?

Power.

Remember that Harry Potter was a baby Witch (albeit a strong blood Witch) and like Ron and Hermione had to go to school to learn to heighten and master his innate magical gifts.

Which we all have FYI.

But Dumbledore didn't even need his wand. Sure he used it to amplify his power but he was the most powerful of all and that power stemmed from inside him and THROUGH the wand. So the wand was helpful but not needed.
Change of banners anyone?
With one clap he made magic happen.

So what makes a Witch powerful and another weak?

Power in the third dimension comes from confidence, strength and self-love. It comes with a still pure mind set and a passion like thunder.

When you believe in yourself then your magic is strong. Endora on the old series *BeWitched* just raised her hand and storms brewed around her. No tools no dancing just her own force.

You can't be a powerful Witch without being a powerful person.

Chapter 35
Earthing

This is a huge subject and I beseech you to study it more or watch a documentary on the science behind EARTHING or grounding.

We live and grow on this planet but we are the only species that does so without touching the ground or waters.
Oh yes we hover over it in our apartment building and cars or with our rubber soles but we don't connect.

This lack of connection is making humanity sick. The sun feeds us negative ions directly through our feet through the grass, soil or sand or ocean and that's the way we get our life force. Science folks not hearsay.

Part of power is health. To maintain and thrive on the planet I highly recommend putting your feet, body and hands on the ground for a minimum of twenty minutes a day.
Walk barefoot.
Lie in the sand.
Swim in a lake, river or ocean.
Sit in the grass.
Yes, hug that darn tree!!

The life force is a connection to source itself. There are too many studies to quote now but if you are ill or imbalanced get out and lie on the grass naked now!!!

One lady lost fifty pounds in six months just lying in the grass. That's how powerfully grounding or Earthing can pull you back into your divine center.
In the center we are born perfect and divine like the jaguar. Born to thrive and be all that we are capable of.
Jaguars don't lose their balance and they don't gain weight, they stay in their divine form.
So if you are imbalanced in anyway you need grounding more than ever.
Please know dear magical one that your default setting is perfection.

You don't need to fight to get back to what your body default is – you just have to get out of the way and let it return to normal.

Earthing does this for you. Nature is the highest frequency and you can make it heal you and empower your magic.

For me it's just reminded me of the simple fact we all know inside – it just feels better when we connect with nature!!
Again forgive me when so much of this seems simple and logical but – when is the last time you put your feet REALLY on the ground?
I know when I do I just feel better. Peaceful.

Last week I walked to the beach barefoot and plopped my body on the sand by the ocean. A big storm was brewing on the horizon. The waves were pounding, the surf was extreme and the sound was deafening.

I sat beside the water's edge and gloried in the passion of the storm and the power of the ocean. My feet felt chilled but caressed as I dipped them into tempest and the wind whipped my hair into a mess.
It was one of the most joyous feelings I've had in a very long time. The Kardashian reruns can't compete with that.
Moreover as we continue to expand our energy, grounding and keeping our channel connected to the Earth is important to staying balanced.
Roots first my darling magical beings. Suck up power from the feet first and also have more fun.

"We are reaching for the sky and even if we're willows
We still need deep roots."

Building Power with Self Love

Most of my students have no problem getting their dreams manifesting – the problem is bringing it into the third-dimension where they can touch it or feel it.

Why? Because they are baby Witches and need to learn? Yes, partly but the truth is we often block ourselves because of lack of love patterns we've buried since birth and childhood. The third-dimension is brutal at first for a magical being. Gravity, taxes, age and death ouch! That only happens in the third-dimension!

The first dimension is a dot. The second dimension is a line and it isn't until the third-dimension that the TRIANGLE appears and thus

we can materialize a body and things.
The holy trinity then takes on more meaning.

So here we are a bunch of fabulous magical spirits squished into bodies at the lowest dimension that materialization is possible. Please know that only the bravest and most powerful beings are able to manifest themselves into this dimension to begin with!
Well done you!

You are powerful or you wouldn't be here. I need you to understand how awesome you are to even be in the third dimension.
It's as if you are an astronaut that has been sent on a mission to the farthest regions of the galaxy where communication gets iffy and even the realization of your whole expanded self is not possible because of the forgetfulness of this realm. That's what's going on with you in the third dimension.

So how do you love yourself?
This may be why you're reading this book right now- despite all the info I'm channeling and dropping – if you can fix your innate self worth issues and lack of self-love issues you will be unstoppable.

This is one of the easiest and fastest ways to install a love program in yourself instead of what you got stuck with. Because we are patterned when we are young – just sucking in information – we also take in a bunch of lies and misinformation about ourselves. This is where the problem starts.
I worked for years as a spiritual counselor in a high end Malibu rehab with the best program money could buy. When I spoke with our Harvard psychologist about clearing old tapes he said that his profession was limited. Yes he could get a client in the rehab to discover the initial incident that may have affected their self-love in their youth – but finally unearthing the horrible issue didn't change anything.

There was no slap on the head or light bulbs going off that freed the person and self worth and empowerment came flooding in. NO.
It didn't heal anything just knowing.

The only thing I found that works is to be the master of your own destiny and reprogram yourself with the use of mass affirmations to override your faulty program from youth.

Chapter 36

CLEARING OLD TAPES

The most important spell you need to learn is the one that helps you love yourself. I know it sounds cheesy but stay with me - this is just not feel good advice.

Love of self empowers your force.

Self-love or the lack of it affects all areas of your life. Much of what you find missing or flawed in your life is directly connected to how you feel about yourself and if you love yourself.
In my practice I have found that 98% of people I know or have worked with do not love themselves. Even having celebrity fame or millions of dollars does not create self-love.

It may be the third dimension itself is so dark and troubled that the overlay on us as children makes us feel that this is somehow part of us, and then we judge it bad and the unloving begins.

I'm going to give you a simple spell right now.
Close your eyes and take a deep breath and ask yourself this question.

"If I really loved myself what would I do right now?"

If you have a problem or wish an answer on how to proceed in your daily life you can again apply this same simple self-asking. For example: You wonder if you should stay in your current job. Now ask again –

"If I really loved myself what would I do right now?"

SPELL TO LOVE YOURSELF

The first premise to building power in yourself and your craft is to allow yourself to love yourself, crooked parts and all. Of course you are already loved beyond measure but in the third dimension we get lost and lose our home light.
We forget we are loveable and we lose our power.
We feel we are somehow not worthy and in this thought we lose our power.
These are lies. These are the lies of the third dimensional darkness. Each soul is a perfect expression of creation with the power to create inherent in them. So too are you filled with divine source throughout this matter filled body.

The only and best way I've found to clear all the unloving programs installed in your third dimensional self you are going to have to reprogram yourself by OVERWRITING your limited and false three-D program.

You can so this easily but it most be done daily and often as your old pattern is deep and easily fallen into.

YouTube is a magical and free resource you can access right now to help you put in a new and higher frequency program of power and love.

I highly recommend using Louise Hays mass affirmations on self-love and self worth. She has free playlists all over YouTube to use and all you need do is listen to the loving affirmations repeated to you.
You can cook or do laundry or anything as long as you can hear it in the background.
Try and listen to two hours of self-love affirmation vids everyday.

THIS ALONE WILL BRING YOU GREAT JOY AND POWER!

I know this sounds a bit cliché and easy but it is so important. If we want to be powerful we have to create things and allow them in to the third dimension. If we don't love ourselves we block that magic from appearing. And then we judge ourselves.

So take dear Robin Williams, he seemingly had everything. He created magic in his life and on screen no doubt. He had millions of adoring fans and a loving wife. What he didn't have was love for himself.
When you have it all – but the most important love then it just magnifies the sense of lack and sadness.
You feel as if what is the point of living.
And thus my insistence on building the foundation of your craft from the most important cornerstone of all – SELF LOVE.

In my practice is I work with all sorts of successful people that sadly also like most of us humans got the faulty unloving program.
There are many video artists with self-love affirmation compilations. Choose one that makes you feel good to listen to. Again I always recommend Louise Hays affirmations because she is so incredibly

high frequency and powerful and if you listen to her mass self love affirmations daily you will finally rewrite your own program.
Thee old faulty program of unworthiness will be replaced by new loving thoughts as the new program settles in and you listen daily. Soon you will just love yourself despite what you think now or anyone else tries to make you believe otherwise.
You will trust that you are worthy and loveable just because you are.

No one is perfect we are all crooked sticks my dear ones. Embrace your uniqueness, strive for greatness and know you deserve it.

MIRROR WORK

A daily ritual you can do to enhance your love of self is to look in the mirror and tell yourself you love yourself. Do this when you look like crap and when you are looking your best.

Look yourself in the soul of your eyes and remind yourself how awesome you are. What a divine magical and special being you are. I love you!

Daily Easy Sticky Note Spell

Get a pack of sticky notes. Write the most wonderful fabulous compliments you can think of on each piece of notepaper.
Now take the notes and randomly paste them around the house in funny places like on the milk carton in your fridge or your toilet seat. For certain put some of the sticky notes on your mirrors so you see them around you.
Throughout the day you will run into these high frequency messages and like a little calling from the divine remind you that you are indeed AWESOME and magical.

Chapter 37 How to Talk to Angels, Deities, Animals andthe Deceased.

O ne part of being a magical person is the ability to talk to the other side. Be it a deceased person or an Angelic prophet, deity or aliens for that matter.
Spirit communication occurs through our shared space and decoding messages sent to our sixth sense.

Sixth Sense Communication

If you've never sent or gotten messages through your sixth sense of vibration before they can be different from what you might expect. Sometimes message have to be deciphered because messages often come in symbols.

Part of learning to speak to Angels, animals or the dead means having to work on those skills that you may not have used in the past. The number one tool to prepare your mind for listening and understanding all beings is meditation and I'll guide you through that later.

Angels, deities and those that have passed over do not always speak to you in English or whatever language you speak. In my experience I've never heard some weird ghostly voice or alien language.

Disembodied spirits speak to us with the universal language and communicate to us by using the space, which is the universal connector in a way that we can understand.
They speak by projecting images and sometimes-whole conversations directly into your mind. They all speak through direct vibrational transference so you feel it in your gut.

In other words, you won't be listening to these beings with your ears or speaking with your mouth. You will be directing your communication directly through ESP if you will. Mental or spirit telepathy.

I will remind you again that you are born with this sixth sense ability. Now we will begin to understand how it works FOR YOU.

The sixth sense is a communication device that will help you speak and understand others in whatever form they may be.

Angels, spirits, and deities all communicate differently but they all use your sixth sense to speak.

Chapter 38 Honing Your Gift Through Meditation

W arning - you're not going to like this part.
This is where the discipline part comes in. Nobody likes discipline. But no great character or anything of value is achieved without discipline.
Discipline brings power.

Even if you had no desire to communicate with disembodied entities Meditation is still one of the best things you can do to have the happiest life possible.
It helps the junk fall away and your true path to bliss be revealed to you.

So many people don't know that the quickest way to understand who you are and what will make you happy – all of you, which is composed of your mind, your body, and your spirit - is through meditation.

OK I hear the groans. I got you. I'm one of those people that hated and avoided meditation.

Seemingly sitting and not doing anything has never been my thing. However here is the good news.

I found out that I could actually trick myself into discipline if I started with *ten minutes a day*.

TEN MINUTES A DAY

Anyone can manage ten minutes a day.
Truly that is all you need.

Ten minutes a day to focus on universal connection – so you can tell the difference between YOUR OWN VOICES and OTHER VOICES. Your own pictures and symbols that mean something.

So you can clear your head of clutter to better SEE if that's your best sense.

Or to just FEEL what is going on with your natural gift of clairsentience.

You can only craft these gifts by spending time being in the space and being quiet enough to first learn your own head and voices that barrage your mind so that when *another voice* comes in we know that IT IS another voice because it is not yours. (Or vision or feeling.)

Luckily once you get going and consistent with your meditation for ten minutes you will stop resisting it and sometimes you may wish to go longer and stay in the meditative place.

This is very beneficial you could be getting some really good information in this space.
I often get my entire books downloaded from the Angelic realm in this space.

Chapter 39

Recognizing Voices in Meditation

Here's the deal, there's no getting around it if you really want to be in tune you need to figure out your own voices or pictures in your own head.

You're going to need to ferret out yourself from the other messages coming to you.

I am using my own experience as a clairaudient. Again you may not hear things, you may see things or get symbolic images or you may feel something or a knowing.

Here's an example - say you want to talk to a relative that's past over to the other side, or an animal that is in your life or past – how will you recognize true communication if you don't know which of the voices in your head are yours and which are not yours?

Thoughts and images and issues can come from the environmental they can come for old programming, they can come from yourself they can come from your fear -so if you don't know which voice of yours is on stage – who knows maybe you have 10 voices or ideas popping up
No judgment -it just makes you schizophrenic - I'm kidding! It means you have a lot of stuff going on inside you that you have pushed under the proverbial rug of life and now you're picking up the edge of the carpet and there it all is.
Until you wade through that part of your mind and psyche that needs a voice and understanding – examine it – feel it – own it and gently let it drift away with your next breath it will not be at peace.

You clear all the past and enter into the present with each breath.

Continue to follow your breath in and out slowly listen to the air moving through your body as if it's breathing you.
Try not to judge yourself when your head starts spitting over every problem you haven't dealt with. This is common in the beginning. We so rarely give ourselves undivided thought attention that when we do sit down to listen sometimes we get an earful for a minute. Expect resistance; sit through it for ten minutes anyway.

Soon and with time you will just sit in the moment in the space of the divine.

Remember the space is the divine connector of all of us.

Remember you're 99.99% divine space. Only a very tiny part of you is made up of atoms or matter - so it really doesn't matter at all and when you become a master you'll realize you can conquer matter with your spirit - but we are in the third dimension so let's just keep going on and not freak anyone out too early.

Meditation 10 minutes a day folks. I recommend the same time every day. You can find some great music on YouTube and also I recommend that you try different cultural music that you may not have experienced before but may be just perfect for you.
I like double shamanic drumming to help me enter a trance and really rev up my frequencies.
The drumming is rather advanced and can pull you deep, so if you are a baby Witch you might want to start out with wind chimes, ocean wave sounds or Mayan flutes.

Perhaps silence is what works for you.

The bottom line is *you're getting into a relationship with you and your spirit* and from there you're getting to know yourself and your true soul.
Remember to record what you are learning and experiencing in your *Book of Shadows* so you can go back and reflect later.

But remember we don't want perfect. Folks nobody is perfect. Life is a mess of broken pieces stumbling along falling into failures and ascending to wins and failures again that make the most interesting and amazing people and beautiful life -so if you're *crooked* - welcome to the world of the third dimension!

Chapter 40

Strengthening your Sixth Sense

M oving into the second week of meditation and what you should expect.

So after two weeks of you sitting down and committing to 10 minutes of meditating you got a find that your brain your spirit and body stop fighting you when you go to do it.

At this point they should be less resistant and just be like "whatever 10 minutes let's just do it" and at that point also your mind starts giving you a break and the constant chatter starts to quiet down. You're beginning not to fight the constant thoughts in your head and trying to push back and you're getting into *more of a flow* that involves breath and the space.
That means you're starting to move along and you're learning to get into THE SPACE.

Continuing on with the meditation during these two weeks you're going to continue to deal with your own stuff and wading through the chatter and junk in your head.

A bit of soul cleaning if you will.

All this is great!!!

There is a true sense of peace when you start dealing and listening to all parts of yourself.

Healing on all levels begins here.

So when a thought comes in acknowledge the thought, and then it let it go slowly– imagine putting it inside a big pink bubble and then lovingly letting it go up to the sky – see it getting smaller and smaller until it's gone altogether.
Now focus back on the breath.
WE are trying to get to silence in this part of the work – having acknowledged the voices in the first two weeks now lets try and let them go so we can just BE in the space.
Try and focus back on the simple inhalation of your breath and exhalation of your breath if you feel lost or too many thoughts crowd in too quickly.

A lot of people like to sit in the Lotus position, which is a loose cross-legged position with your hands on your legs.

I sit like this because if I lay down I tend to get sleepy.
But honestly try different things because we're all unique beings here and you need to find what works best for the amazing spirit that is you!
I think the sitting lotus position keeps you alert and it keeps your energy running through your body so I would recommend that.

Continue to write down anything that comes up during your meditation – especially concentrating on any intense feelings that came up. You may get pictures, feelings or hear things so make sure you keep a record of all of them in your Book of Shadows.

Chapter 41

Angels and Deities

The more I've worked with wise caring spirits the more I've had to expand what Angel means to me. When I speak of Angels it brings most people to the Christian version of Angels.

I believe now that any divine being holding love and good will that cares to help me is an Angel. Aphrodite and Trees both qualify as Angels in my world, as do some of the ancient Gods and Goddesses that have offered assistance to humans.
This is my perception. Again what you believe is valid for YOU. Be you. Be unique and create a magic practice that works with your beliefs.
(I'm a recovering Catholic yet I still use Jesus in all my workings.)

We all have guardian Angels.

We each have at least two assigned to us. One that sits on the left and right side of us for protection and guidance.
Depending on your soul mission and actions you may draw more Angels or spirit guides to you and even power animals that are like Animal Angels to protect and lend strength to our human self and the service asked of us.

You may feel drawn to work with a certain deity and want to connect to them. If you want to connect to with a particular deity, Angel or spirit than I always start with a protection prayer as well.
I use my Super Prayer, which I've already listed.

At this point you can ask through your mind to have your Angels or the deities you'd like to communicate with to reveal themselves to you or help you in some way.
Ascended Masters and spirit voices come to me in different forms. PLEASE NOTE! This is how it works for me. Things may occur very different for you that have meaning for you.

Spirits are quite aware we don't believe in them and they seek often to give you reliance in some way that they are in fact real. This can occur in multiple ways and always personal to you in some way.

Angels are not people (some have had human experiences) and they have very different personalities and teaching strategies.
If you are a strict Catholic Angels may show up in a form you expect them to look like. They take form in a way that is not them but a projection of them that you can relate to most easily.
My teacher Angel White Eagle shows up in the form of a Mohawk Chief and my other Angel is a kick ass Goddess named Saraswati who is an Indian deity (have no idea how I got involved with her) she is a ball buster folks!!
Saya insists I burn through all my blocks NOW.

When I complain, because you know us humans we hate change especially quick change – her response is always
"Oh would you like to wait another life time to get over this Goddess?"
She always calls me Goddess for some reason and then asks for chocolate.
She also always insults my sloppy dressing.
"Goddess of all the things on the planet THIS is what you choose?"
Obviously she's never known the comfort of loose fitting sweat pants!
The point is Angels and deities have their own personalities. White Eagle is calm and patient and Sayaswati is not!

I have also found that they are often funny.
If you find yourself the butt of the joke – congratulations you've hit the high frequency Angel crowd! They are not sulking around all serious in white gowns they are souls with personalities! They are more smiling like the Buddha – again especially I noticed when I have a major fail – foot in the mouth etc. they think it is hysterical. Not very Angelic actions -but you know what – a heck of a lot more fun!!!! I guess comedy is appreciated in all dimensions.

Also I notice Angels and deities use weird vocabulary that you have in your data banks (they can only access what you know and have learned and stored in your brain.)

No weird alien I language is going to pop up, but if suddenly you hear a voice in your head talking and it says 'ERGO' and you ask yourself - "Ergo? Who the heck says that anymore?"
ANGELS and deities do.
They don't know ERGO is an outdated word so they use it if its correct - so look and listen for that. Weird usage of words or the melody or cadence in which they deliver it.
Also Angels whisper they don't scream –

Unless you get Saya coming your way than look out she's going to be heard no matter what!
Love her!

I have also noticed with high entity beings – I spoke to the Sphinx once – and it communicated an entire conversation in a downloaded triangle all at once. The conversation seemed to be transferred complete in a downloaded triangle form and I had to in essence unroll it and then unroll it and read/listen to it linearly left to right so I could understand.

Angels, prophets and divine beings seem to be much more chatty than other spirits. I believe it is because they are trying to help the planet and us. I mean – I've written six books with the Angels worth of stuff to say!

Other disembodies beings don't seem to have as long of conversations with me personally. As far as my deceased friends and family they show up more with a supportive or loving message, which are usually brief.

That said, I had no regrets with any of my loved ones that have passed - you may need to settle feelings or arguments that were not dealt with on Earth and you may have longer conversations.

This is my heads up however my dear magical aspirant.
When you're entering other realms you're *vulnerable* it's just true you're leaving your body you're doing different things that might bend your mind body and spirit in a wonderful exciting way but also I've seen people have some negative repercussions if they go to far to fast.

Let's be real – unless you are strong mind body and spirit DO NOT go hanging in the doorway of the third dimension if you can't hold on. That door way is also an exit.

I've had people have near death experience next to me and White Eagle kicked in gear and had me push their spirits back in through their heart chakra – they were in the Mayan Ruins, doing mushrooms and they
lost their triangle – what happens when you lose your triangle geometry? STRAIGHT LINE folks.
Dead.
There is a reason the American Indians prayed and fasted before they went to commune with the GREAT WHITE SPIRIT.
They just didn't drop a bunch of drugs and say hey lets go hang on the doorway of death and peek out of the third dimension –
GO SLOW.

I've seen others so spooked by leaving their body or getting too close to the universal all that they start addictions again or lose themselves in a bad relationship because they've gone too far too fast. Usually with hallucinogenic drugs (which I'm not against in shamanic experiences but that's a whole other book).

The bottom line this is not a race. You can go slowly. If you feel unbalanced or scared or stressed just STOP. Relax and wait until you feel called to work on your connection again.

Everything is all right. You don't have to do anything that makes you feel bad. Only move ahead when all parts of you are excited and ready to expand.

Again this is not a race. You got this far already! Bravo you!!!
Just the fact you allowed your mind to be bent in another direction and your spirit to explore another path is commendable!! You are amazing and naturally magical never forget it!

Chapter 42 Trust

So what do I mean by trust?
I mean trust you actually are getting communication albeit in a form you never have or allowed before.
Trust. That things are more magical than you might have thought and maybe talking to Angels, animals and dead people isn't so strange. Maybe it's inherent in our DNA.

Trust. That your mind has better things to do then burp up a memory from Victorian days for no reason. If you're getting a strange message - trust it.
Trust that the work you've done to quiet your mind has allowed your gifts and truths to be uncovered and honed.
TRUST. You can do it because you can.
What's really happening is you've actually stepped up and connected yourself to divine energy. Okay here comes a big one

trust almost always I found that we've been getting psychic messages all the time and we don't trust them.

When I went through hypnotherapy and got regressed to my childhood I discovered that psychic messages come like real memories come and it's almost like they flicker by and if I wasn't under hypnosis I might wonder if I wasn't lying! In truth we get psychic messages like this all the time and we discount them.

Perhaps you're walking through town and you're like "Oh this feels like when I was back in Egyptian times or like I was here before…"

Guess what? Just the fact *that you felt that is real,* your brain is not burping up some stupid stuff out of nowhere it is trying to communicate with you –"Hey man you lived here that's why it feels familiar!"

That's trust. Trust is the difference between people that are gifted intuitive or not

Chapter 43

Talking to Animals

Gosh don't we love animals! They truly are some of our true Earth Angels and hold the highest divine energy of love. Animals help also help us clear our aura and balance our energy. Like trees, and lakes and flowers - animals are a gift to our world and our connection to them is sacred.

Animals don't speak human. Obvious. But just like the Angels – they can communicate with you through telepathy. If a darling fur baby you love has passed over to the other side you can still connect and communicate with them just as you can with other disembodies spirits.

The body is a third dimensional vehicle but our total selves are 99.99 is light so we change and create but we never die. The matter part may transform but it is really minute.

Please know that your animals that have passed over know that you love them and are still nearby you always.

You can communicate with them through your mind spirit connection.

Remember as you work on this you will get better at it. If you feel frustrated or that you are not getting anything you feel is validated –

Ask the ANGELS or guides to help you and then continue on.

Through meditation and your true desire to connect you will be shown that you are indeed communicating with your pet that has passed.

Some day there will be a message or symbol and you will know that there is no way you could have made it up. THIS will validate your gift for you. But please know your gift is valid now.

Yes you will get better at deciphering the way messages come through you, and you will start to trust more.

It's as simple as clearing your head – asking a question or listening to what comes in when you question your animal (or a passed animal.)

If you are trying to connect to a living animal, clear your head and send them a message through pictures, mental words or feelings.

Wait and clear your mind and see if you get something in return.

Remember this will take a moment to perfect because you haven't used it your whole life –and moreover most likely didn't believe you could do it!

Take time, trust and keep working at it. With time you will succeed I promise!

Chapter 44 Wild Animal Messengers

Sometimes wild random animals will appear in our lives out of the blue. Maybe a bunny jumps across your path or a deer runs by etc. Always take a moment to clear your head after such an encounter and see if that animal came into your sphere to send you a message.

Red cardinals for instance have always been a symbol from a loved one that has passed and is saying hello.

Hawks are known to bring messages from the ancients.

Animals often show up to give us messages.

If a bird starts squawking at you out of the blue – LISTEN.

Get quiet and see what thoughts form in your head. What is the bird trying to say?

Maybe nothing.

Maybe he's hungry and has nothing to do with you.

Maybe.

Or maybe you don't trust yourself enough yet to believe what you're hearing in your mind could be a bird communicating with you. It's okay babes. It takes time to get used to being a weirdo that can communicate with animals.

Understand Animal Messages

Say you just don't understand the message you are getting or it makes no sense.
First – ask for clarity. See if more information comes forward.

Second – consider this may be a sign or metaphor that does not make sense directly or YET.

Third – Look around you for extra signs and clues to what the original message may have meant. Realize that sometimes things are not literal they are prompts to get you to remember something – for instance an inside joke that only you know or a memory that something jogs your brain and delivers the answer you were looking for.

Chapter 45

Power Animals

Did you know animals have tribes or clans? So the clan of felines the clan of bears etc.

When you do something kind for an animal, rescue a kitten; donate to save the whales etc. – the soul tribe of that animal is aware.

Often they will in turn unite with you and send a special animal guide to gift you there power – say the lion – strength, leadership, good hair!

As a way of saying thank you. It's truly beautiful to work with the clan energy and I'm very excited for you to understand and participate with these Angelic beings because animals are Angels too.

One way the animal clan will let you know you have a gift guide coming is through a DREAM or in real life the same animal shows itself to you in *three ways it is a signal* they are aligning themselves with you as a power animal and you can use their gifts.

So it can be either three tigers in your dream or the same tiger you see from three different views or three times in the same dream. This is the shamanic sign that they want to join with you and gift you their animal power.

Congratulations!! Animal Angels are amazing and often come for only a window of time to help with a certain event. Thus they lend you their power to help you.

Now power animals are not your totem animals that are always the same and stay with you like your guardian Angels – power animals come to help for a certain reason.

When I was in the rainforest the jaguar came to me and well that's a whole other book!

In any case our connection with animals is so deep and fruitful and good for our hearts – here on Earth and everywhere after we may travel.

Chapter 46 Talking to the Dead

N ow lets talk about communicating with people who have passed over. This is the easiest.

Dear friend if you have lost someone then please take solace in knowing that they are not gone. Their spirit is infinite and you already have a soul contract with any family or close friend that has passed and will always be near each other.

These people will never leave you for all time. They are your soul family and will travel with you throughout time.

Yes they may leave the Earth party sooner than you but they have not disappeared – they are just at a party across town or time if you will. YOU will meet again in full spirit form someday but currently you are stuffed into a little material body in the third dimension. That doesn't mean they aren't with you always.

Unlike the limitation of the third dimension, age, death, and gravity – your expanded spirit self can travel and be in multiple places at once.

Your loved ones are always near you because they love you and are protecting you – even if part of them is busy building a star system or something else.

Because love is the strongest frequency it can never end nor die - so despite not being able to see your loved one that has passed you still 'have their number' if you will. That means anytime you can call them up – Still.

The way you call them up is in your mind.

Again look around and see what's being shown to you. If something reminds you of a person that has passed – know that is them reaching out and waving at you!

They're saying "I'm here right beside you we're still close you just can't see me."

People you have loved always are there. You can speak to them anytime you want. Talk in your mind and then listen to the response in your mind.

Now at first- you're not going to trust yourself.

You're not going to believe you are not just "Making up the conversation" to fool yourself.

Maybe you think your nuts.

I say take a deep breathe and just have that whole conversation. I talk to my deceased friends and family all the time. Oddly – and again here comes that comedy jokes on me thing – they love to want to start up a conversation when I'm on the toilet at night.

How uncouth.

I think they think it's funny.

Maybe it's just quiet.

In any case. Every night I'm having a quick chat with someone on the other side.

Personally I do not like to talk to random dead people I don't know.

I will do that if a person needs healing and relief from sadness but in general I only want to talk to my dead peeps and if I want advise I don't go to my dead friends or relatives I go HIGHER!

I go to the Angels!

Let's be clear if your stupid but sweet Uncle Eddy dies he's not suddenly Einstein or Archangel Michael – *he's still stupid sweet Uncle Eddy with a slightly better view.*

So if you just fancy a chat, or to hang out get family advise from Uncle Eddy that's all good.

However if you want life lessons or major destiny answers – I beseech you go HIGHER FREQUENCY.

Angels, Jesus, the Four Elements that kind of higher divine energy NOT SWEET UNCLE EDDY!

Chapter 47 Ghosts and Spirits

S omehow I got into ghost busting. It's nothing I wanted to do, but it is a sacred mission I've been sent on several times.

Oddly after I won the scholarship to the rainforest to be in the Mayan ruins it seemed as if some big light bulb turned on inside me and I started getting approached by ghosts.

Weird, I know. Not anything I went to college for and certainly nothing I wanted as a career. But life has a way of making me the butt of its joke and now here I am teaching you how to reach across the divide and communicate as well.

Not so scary, after all. BUT – again, I'm going to emphasize the protection of self and home as I continue with this chapter of unwanted or unknown entities contacting you because you're light is on.

Spirits can see who's light is on like an old-time phone booth. Your aura pops through the dimensions, and you GLOW.
I might add this glow is a heart glow. It will also make you beautiful inside and out because your spirit is glowing, and there is no vitamin for that.

However, some strange and sometimes scary things happen when you do TURN ON. If you decide to use your gift in service to humanity, then you may find yourself approached by ghosts of dead people you don't know.
Let me begin with – don't worry. If you don't want to deal with disembodied spirits, then it's your right. You can do whatever you want. You are in charge, and you set boundaries.

I do not deal with any run-of-the-mill spirits unless they were human and are now stuck, and then I'm in service doing a soul retrieval. But random spirits?
No thanks, not for me. They don't register on my radar because I will it to be so.
I work with the highest masters possible, so I get information from the highest vibrational energy possible. I do recommend this.
There are just random spirits out there though and nasty ones too if that's what you desire to connect with. Just remember, you are in charge and also to be clear about what you want, aka clear intention.
If you feel weird, bad, or afraid, repeat the protection prayer, send the energy away, and then call on Christ's power to fill your body and room. You can use the protection prayer in the chapter on protecting yourself during spirit encounters. Again if the use of Christ is not for you, choose whatever you believe represents ultimate protection for you.

Ghosts

I don't see ghosts, nor hear them – I FEEL ghosts. As I've mentioned, I'm a clairaudient channel for Angels, and hearing is what I count on when I'm connecting – BUT, also, I'm not particularly eager to get creeped out.

Usually, when I walk into a room or home with a ghost, I feel it right away. A presence or energy is typically uncomfortable or heavy. Sometimes when I sleep, I wake and feel pressure as if someone has sat next to me.

.

I don't like to be bothered while I sleep, and nighttime ghost busting is not for me. I'm keen to help, but it is a choice.

I don't like to be approached by random energies in the middle of the night, so I make very clear to the spirits – *talk to me in the morning AFTER my second coffee, and I'm keen to be of service.*

Boundaries people.
Good on Earth - Good EVERYWHERE.
Know what your boundaries are and assert them gently and with mutual respect but always protect yourself.

Dealing with ghosts is a true holy mission because you are helping a soul find its way home to its soul tribe and full light.

When they are split, they are broken, and they cling to what they knew as a human.

Purgatory, if you want to name it that – seems to me from what the spirits have told to be a bus stop where the bus never comes. So they are always waiting.

The soul that is passed usually has forsaken their belief in anything divine or an afterlife. They no longer believe or never believed the truth of their soul. So they don't want to let go of their human reality, and they CLING on to what they know. Objects – homes often. It's important to realize that no other being is keeping that soul in this suspended state (purgatory, if you will).

The soul itself is choosing to cling to its former life because the soul is in fear.

Fear is purgatory.

These spirits need help.

Every ghost I've ever dealt with needs the same thing.
They don't believe in an afterlife. They only believe in humanity and what they know. So they only trust humans.
That's why they come to you or me if you come across a ghost.
They need to be told it's okay to go to the light and let go of their human body by a human.
They need to be told it's better and beautiful, and they are hurting themselves with the fear of the unknown despite the fact they are living a non-life—a ghost of a life.
The souls need to be reminded all the people who love them are waiting for them to have the strength to let go and – here comes that word again – TRUST.
Whenever I feel a ghost or face a ghost, I always start with my protection prayer first.
Then I clear my mind and ask the spirit ghost what's going on. Often they don't know, so don't expect some brilliant litany of reasons, and they don't know what's wrong, which is why they are coming to you.

Tell them that God/the Universe and their family loves them.
We all go back to the source and come from the source and back again like tides in the ocean.
Tell them to let go and be happy.
Sometimes it takes a while.
If I leave a situation and days later, I'm still thinking about that spirit, and I say another prayer, send them good thoughts and keep urging them onward to happiness.
At some point, I stop thinking about them, and that's when I know they have passed on to the vibration of light and are finally free.

Amen.

Chapter 48
Simple Useful Spells

The most useful magic is the kind we create everyday. It is in these daily rituals we feel our true connection to our own soul and true power. Here are some easy beginner spells that may be useful to you. I encourage you to make up your own spells to suit your needs and life. In the end, becoming present in your own life is the greatest gift you can give yourself and others.

New Moon Money Magic

What you need:
5 Dollar Bills
(Or 5 nickels etc.)

Put the money in front of you and confront it as if it were employees that worked for you.
Say this spell:

I send you out to work today
Round up the cash and send it my way
Gather your friends and bring them to me
lots of money I soon will see.

Now go out and spend all the money you just said the words over. They will go out and find more and bring it back to you.

Good Morning Spell

What you need:
Morning sun
You in bed

When you first wake up in the morning and you are still not quite awake. Before you open your eyes say this spell:

I greet this day all brand new
I'm happy, healthy and abundant too.

Now open your eyes and get out of bed and face the sun. Smile and know you are going to have a wonderful day.

Wash Away Troubles

What you need:
Shower or bath or Ocean

Get inside the water. Feel the water surround and comfort you. Never forget you are 80% water and the water is you.

Feel the water inside of you connecting to the water around you.

Say these words:

Oh beautiful water that I love
Surround and touch me like a glove
I am safe and happy and free
Clean and clear so let it be.

To Bring Love to You

What you will need:

A picture of the person you love (or write their name on a piece of paper)
Something they have owned, or touched, or dirt from the ground they walked over.
New moon
A flower seed
A pot of soil

On the new moon gather all your things together and sit on the floor as the moon rises.
Take out your pot of soil and dig a hole down deep. Place the picture of name of the one you love in the soil. Cover it up with an inch of soil and put the seed on top of this.

Say this spell:

Oh love of mine that I do know
I bid our love to grow and grow
As this seed grows up from the bottom
So our relationship now will blossom.
So mote it be.

Now water the seed lightly and put it on your windowsill or someplace that will get sunshine for it to grow. Take care of your plant as it grows and know that so too shall your enchantment grow in the mind of your lover for you.

To Bring Health to a Friend

What you need:
A picture of the friend, or write their name on a piece of paper.
A white candle

Sit in front of the picture of your friend or family that needs better health or good wishes. Light the candle and say their name three times.

Then say this spell.

I see you (insert name) well and happy and strong
I see you playing all day long
Healthy, wealthy and joyful too
Only good things will come to you.
So mote it be

The Great Calling

So my friends we find ourselves at the end of this magical instruction.
I thank you for turning on your power.

When you manifest the things you love you bring joy to yourself and the world!! When you take the time to fill your own cup soon you will be overflowing with gifts.
Thank you for working on your divine ability and awakening the miracles and magic in you!

I hope that when your magic is in full power and you have all the things any human could desire that you join me and other light workers around the globe to use our magic to help heal the world.

We are in the middle of a great evolution and we need all of you wonderful magical people to turn on and help.
You can do this daily by sending love and gratitude to the planet everyday as part of your practice.
In Lakesh my dear magical being.
I am another yourself.
Thank you for spending time with me great one.

Wishing you high frequencies!

Printed in Great Britain
by Amazon